RIDING THE DRAGON

RIDING THE DRAGON

Managing Your Chinese Investors Partners and Employees

CT JOHNSON

2016

Copyright © 2016 by CT Johnson

All rights reserved. This book or any portion thereof may not be reproduced or used in any manner whatsoever without the express written permission of the publisher except for the use of brief quotations in a book review or scholarly journal.

Limit of Liability/Disclaimer of Warranty: This document provides general information which is current at the time of production. The information contained in this document does not constitute advice and should not be relied on as such. Although the author has endeavored to provide accurate and timely information, there can be no guarantee that such information is accurate as of the date it is received and that it will continue to be accurate in the future. The advice and strategies contained herein may not be suitable for your situation. Professional advice should be sought prior to any action being taken in reliance on any of the information. Cross Border Management and CT Johnson disclaim all responsibility and liability (including, without limitation, for any direct or indirect or consequential costs, loss or damage or loss of profits) arising from anything done or omitted to be done by any party in reliance, whether wholly or partially, on any of the information. Any party that relies on the information does so at its own risk.

First Printing: 2016

ISBN 978-1-326-52503-3

www.crossbordermanagement.com
www.ct-johnson.com

Contents

Acknowledgements	vii
Introduction	1
The Model	9
Customers, Investors and Bosses	19
Problem # 1 – Wanting The World	23
Problem # 2 – Being Treated Like A Child	27
Problem # 3 – Drinking To Excess	31
Problem # 4 – Not Our Expertise	37
Problem # 5 – Being All Things	41
Problem # 6 – Bad Deals	45
Problem # 7 – Saying Yes	49
Problem # 8 – Being Mistreated	53
Problem # 9 – Being Closely Watched	57
Problem # 10 – Constant Effort	61
Problem # 11 – Ignored Suggestions	65
Problem # 12 – Underlying Meanings	69
Problem # 13 – Lack Of Clarity	73
Problem # 14 – Proving Yourself	77
Problem # 15 – Being Suspect	81
Problem # 16 – Friends & Family	85
Problem # 17 – Time Wasting	89

Peers & Partners — 97

- Problem # 18 – Being Cheated — 99
- Problem # 19 – Finding Fault — 103
- Problem # 20 – Getting The Gist — 107
- Problem # 21 – Unshared Wisdom — 111
- Problem # 22 – Friends Like These — 115
- Problem # 23 – Untrustworthy — 119
- Problem # 24 – The Greasy Pole — 123

Employees, Subordinates & Vendors — 129

- Problem # 25 – Father Figures — 131
- Problem # 26 – Unchallenging — 135
- Problem # 27 – A Black Box — 139
- Problem # 28 – Hidden Meanings — 143
- Problem # 29 – Unfaithful — 147
- Problem # 30 – Widely Educated — 151

What Happens Next? — 157
Conclusion — 161
How To Reach CT — 162
About The Author — 163

Acknowledgements

I would like to thank a number of people for their contributions to this book. As this is not the Academy Awards, I've chosen not to limit myself in who made the list.

My Friends In China

I'd like to thank Leroy Blimegger, for sharing his experience as an expatriate living in China and his observations about Chinese culture; John Bould, for his encouragement and for acting as a sounding board when we were both trying to understand something about China; Ling Bould, for helping me get started when I first went out on my own in China; Fan Chang, for his relentless support, encouragement and clear explanations of the Chinese view of the world; Anders Karlsbourg, for sharing his experience as an expatriate living in China and his observations about Chinese culture; Jason Li, for keeping me engaged when I was feeling overwhelmed; Sabrina Meng, for giving me my first job in China; Guo Ping, for being so accessible and helpful, and for the horseback riding; Peng Bo, for his example as a leader and for his genius at bridging the gap between Chinese and Western cultures; Shen Hui, for daring to tell me when I was making mistakes and helping me to do better; Joseph Smith, for sharing his rich experience, for his enthusiasm and for being positive about what's possible; Wu Shuya, for listening to my endless questions about *why* Chinese people do things a certain way; Katie Yao, for hosting me on my first trip to China, and for being my friend ever since; Yi Xiang, for explaining what Chinese bosses want from their employees; and Candice Yu, for her confidence in me and for sharing her considerable experience on both sides of the cultural divide.

My Friends Outside Of China

I'd like to thank Jane Anderson for her excellent marketing advice; Matt Church, Pete Cook and Christina Guidotti, for their individual encouragement, and for the Thought Leaders program they've developed for the benefit of us all; Darren Flemming, for practical tips on writing; Donna McGeorge, for cheerfully pushing me to "write the damned book already"; Georgia Murch for saying writing would be easier than I thought; Andrew Pratley, for pushing me to make the book better; my best friend Scott Sereboff, for 30 years of encouragement; Sun Song, for his patience in explaining so many things about China and for giving me my first introductions there; Glenn Tranter, for his friendship, support and encouragement; James Wagstaff, for constantly returning the conversation to something constructive and useful, no matter how much I whined; and Xia Yan, for her willingness to take on a 40 year-old language student and for infecting me with her passion for China.

My Family

I'd like to thank my mother, Jean, and my brother, Marcus, for thinking writing a book was a cool thing for me to do; my brothers-in-law Pete, John and Bill, for giving me the uniquely Australian praise of "good on ya"; my children, Katherine and Daniel, for demonstrating their approval of the project and affection for me through copious applications of good-natured ribbing; and, most of all, my wife Anne-Marie, who was unremittingly supportive, helpful and encouraging, and without whose help this book would never have been completed.

Thank you all for your patience and guidance, your contributions, your use of the editor's red pen…

Introduction

"It does not do to leave a live dragon out of your calculations, if you live near him."

"The Hobbit," J. R. R. Tolkien

My assumption is that if you've picked up this book, you have a *problem*. You have a Chinese investor who's making your life hell. You have a Chinese boss you find incomprehensible. You have a Chinese partner who's cheating you. You have Chinese employees who are driving you to distraction.

When I'm talking to people about their Chinese business, three types of problems continually come up:

- I'm totally overwhelmed by the demands of dealing with the Chinese.
- I never know what's coming next.
- I'm constantly on the defensive; I never feel like I'm in control.

The thing they often DON'T say, but are nonetheless thinking, is:

- I'm being cheated, but it can't be helped.

That all generates a tremendous feeling of helplessness and frustration.

What's really happening is that your carefully planned and well-executed strategy is being eaten by a 5,000 year-old culture that's different from the one you grew up in. As a senior executive at a large Chinese company said to me, "With China, culture is always there. You can ignore it, but that doesn't help. Your only choice is to go home, or to try and deal with things in a Chinese way."

Riding The Dragon

According to Chinese legend, dragons are ferocious creatures that bring luck and prosperity to those who are strong and disaster to those who aren't. That's a good metaphor for the Chinese side of your business – it can be a powerful force that guides you to fortune or it can be a fire-breathing monster that eats you and everything you possess.

My experience is that Western firms and managers with a Chinese side to their business fall into five broad categories:

Guiding

Riding

Holding Your Own

Retreating

Being Eaten

Guiding – This is where we all want to be, harnessing the power of the Chinese market and using it to make that fortune we've always dreamed of. This is where companies like Bindaree Beef and Hermes live – you're in control of your own destiny and getting exactly what you want out of China. For people in this group, the amount of time you spend managing your Chinese partners isn't excessive and you're happy with the excellent returns you're making. You just need to keep doing what you're doing.

Riding – A step down from guiding is riding; China is taking you where you want to go, but it's messy and you're not in control the way you want to be. Rio Tinto and McGrath Estate Agents are in this category – you're confident that China wants what you have to sell, but your ability to direct that interest or leverage it to expand into new offerings is limited. You spend a significant amount of time managing your Chinese partners and customers, but still value what you're getting out of the relationship enough to be happy with the attention that's required. You just need to refine your approach to managing your Chinese counterparts.

Holding Your Own – If you're in this group, you're wondering what you've gotten yourself into. This is the position that Yahoo is in with Alibaba. You spend half of your available time dealing with problems related to your Chinese customer, investor, boss, partner or operations and regularly wish for an easier life. You rarely feel in control, but see that what you get out of the Chinese side of your business is too valuable to give up. You're over-worked but fundamentally committed to the Chinese business. You need to reevaluate how you're dealing with your Chinese counterparts.

Retreating – People in this group feel things slipping out of control. This is the group that Bear Stearns found itself in with China's CITIC bank. You've lost the initiative to a Chinese counterpart who's constantly making demands of you. You spend an appalling amount of time managing the situation, trying desperately to keep things on a positive track. You feel it's marginal whether to stay engaged with China – things will either improve or you'll exit that part of the business. You badly need to regain the initiative.

Being Eaten – The worst relationship you can have with the dragon is being eaten. If you're in this group, you're tied to your Chinese business in a way that's not easy to dissolve. The highest profile example of this was the acquisition of France's Thomson Electronics, which was acquired by China's TCL, and then lost $100M in market value due to differences in the companies' management styles. You feel you've lost all control in the situation and you spend every waking moment managing your Chinese partners. You need to establish some area – ANY area – where you can exert some control.

I want you to take control of your Chinese business, instead of being controlled by it. By following the strategies outlined in this book, you can spend half as much time dealing with your Chinese counterparts and still get more of what you want out of them.

The Way The Book Works

The book is organized around common problems people have with their Chinese counterparts.

The problems are explained in terms of a model that is set out in the first section of the book. It's kind of a "blue + yellow = green" arrangement that explains what's going on from the Chinese side in terms of cultural beliefs they have and the facts of life in their everyday world. The objective is to help you understand why the Chinese are doing whatever they're doing that's causing you grief. Each section concludes with suggestions about what you can do about the problem.

The problems are grouped into three categories:

- Problems with people to whom you're SELLING (customers, investors and bosses)
- Problems with people with whom you're WORKING (peers and partners)
- Problems with people from whom you're BUYING (vendors and employees)

Above all, this book tries to be three things – simple, useful and relatable. So don't overthink it – go to the parts that look interesting and relevant and don't worry about the rest. Remember to keep it simple. Try to understand the major issues behind the Chinese thinking. Latch on to one or two things you can do to improve the situation. And keep working the problem. The Chinese are in it for the long term. You should be, too.

Section I

The Model

The Model

"Essentially, all models are wrong, but some are useful."

Statistician George E.P. Box

As an American with a professional focus on China, my Western friends often ask me to explain something that's happened in their Chinese business. Usually this is a question about something *bad* that's happened and my friends want to know *what they can do about it*. What can they do about a difficult Chinese partner? What can they do about a sales pitch that failed with a Chinese prospect? What can they do about an unreliable Chinese vendor?

Given the huge differences between Chinese and Western culture, the answer is often complex. Face, hierarchy, different views of time, China's rapidly changing business landscape, massive urbanization, the growth of the Chinese middle class, and outdated views of China in the West all play a part. But my friends don't have time for a lecture about 5,000 years of Chinese history. Frequently they're in the middle of the problem and are just looking for something they can do about it.

To help make sense of these complex issues I've developed a model. It ties business issues to a number of Chinese cultural values and facts of life in China. While the model doesn't explain every facet of Chinese culture, it provides a useful shortcut to understand some of the differences from Western ways of thinking.

The model is comprised of four major elements of Chinese life and culture and eight minor ones.

Major Elements		Minor Elements	
GX	**Guanxi** – Relationships are more important than rules	GP	**Group Orientation** – The group is more important than the individual
HI	**Hierarchy** – All relationships are hierarchical and, thus, unequal	LT	**Long Term Orientation** – The long term is what's most important
FA	**Face** – Face (perception) is more important than facts (reality)	IM	**Incremental Improvement** – Step-by-step improvement is better than revolutionary change
FEU	**Feudalism** – Leadership equals lordship	PR	**Pragmatism** – Don't let perfect be the enemy of good enough
		HA	**Harmony** – Things are better when everyone gets along
		PEO	**People** – China has a HUGE number of people in it
		CRV	**Cultural Revolution** – The Cultural Revolution had a massive impact on society
		RCE	**Rapid Change Environment** – Stuff in China is constantly changing

> The model explains why you can't rely on Western thinking to deal with issues in China. It gives you insights into what your Chinese counterpart is thinking. From there, you can formulate plans that work in a Chinese context.

The four major elements are:
- *Guanxi* (relationships)
- Face
- Hierarchy
- Feudalism

These four elements are at the heart of most problems faced by Westerners in relation to their Chinese business.

<u>Relationships are more important than rules.</u> *"Guanxi"* describes the astonishingly complex and nuanced network of personal relationships that every Chinese person maintains. Guanxi is pervasive and all-encompassing. In many ways, *guanxi* is both overhyped and underappreciated by Westerners who talk about China. *Guanxi* isn't the only force in Chinese culture and it's not a magic potion that makes all things possible. It is, however, ubiquitous and unrelenting. It's a bit like gravity. Gravity doesn't mean that planes always have to stay on the ground, but it does mean that's where they'll end up. Rather than rules, *guanxi* is mostly what guides people's behavior in China. For Chinese people, rules aren't irrelevant, they're simply not as important as personal relationships. *Guanxi* tends to be central to issues surrounding loyalty and trust.

<u>All relationships are hierarchical and, thus, unequal.</u> "Hierarchy" is concerned with people's relative position and authority within the group. Hierarchy mostly

describes the way individuals interact with people who have some kind of power over them (like a boss) or control something the individual wants (like investment or a purchase order). The notion that people are NOT equal is central to the way the Chinese see the world. Hierarchy is usually the driving force behind problems with the way individuals interact with people above them.

△ FA **Face (perception) is more important than facts (reality).** "Face" is a combination of a person's dignity and prestige, and the way they're perceived by the rest of the world. The concept of face is similar to Lee Atwater's axiom that "Perception is reality." For Chinese people, the way things look is just as important as the way they actually are. Face is the driving force behind most problems with communication and appearances.

◯ FEU **Leadership equals lordship.** "Feudalism" is the mirror of hierarchy – it describes the way individuals interact with people over whom they have some power (like employees) or who want something from them (like vendors). The phrase that encapsulates feudalism is "leadership equals lordship," which means that the person in charge has the ability and willingness to exert control, almost a kind of ownership, over the people who answer to them. Feudalism is most often associated with perceptions of unfair treatment.

In addition to the four major elements, there are eight minor cultural elements and facts of life that impact most business relationships;

- Group Orientation
- Long Term Orientation
- Incremental Improvement
- Pragmatism

- Harmony
- People (China's huge population)
- The Cultural Revolution
- China's Rapidly Changing Environment

These elements are most often secondary parts of the explanation as to why the Chinese do things in a particular way, but they're nonetheless important.

△ GP **The group is more important than the individual.** "Group orientation" refers to the fact that the Chinese are much more collective, and place much more importance on the group as a whole, than most European and North American cultures.

△ LT **The long term is what's most important.** "Long termism" is related to the longer view Chinese have about time, as compared to Western societies. For example, the Chinese government publishes Five Year Plans, whereas most governments in the West work on annual budgets.

△ IM **Step-by-step improvement is better than revolutionary change.** "Incremental improvement" describes the preference Chinese people have for step-by-step changes, rather than radical departures from previous ways of working. "Revolutionary" or "radical" improvements are seen as dangerous and undesirable.

△ PR **Don't let perfect be the enemy of good enough.** "Pragmatism" refers to the fact that Chinese businesspeople focus on what can be accomplished quickly and easily, instead of waiting for a perfect solution that may never come. To many Westerners, this can make their Chinese counterparts seem shortsighted and unconcerned with quality.

(HA) <u>Things are better when everyone gets along.</u> "Harmony" is the Chinese quality of placing a premium on the fact that the group itself runs smoothly and that different groups get along with each other. For Chinese people, harmony also has a strong and positive association with stability.

(PEO) <u>China has a HUGE number of people in it.</u> "People" is shorthand for China's huge population, its massive labor pool, and the fact that it's easy for individuals to hide within the larger group (due to the small number of last names and the fact that so many people have moved for work reasons).

(CRV) <u>The Cultural Revolution had a massive impact on society.</u> "Cultural Revolution" refers to the enduring impacts that the Cultural Revolution has had on Chinese society. This is shorthand for the Chinese distrust of people they don't know, their lack of faith in the rule of law, and their obsession with personal loyalty. It's an expression of the negative side of *guanxi*, because it emphasizes what happens in the absence of strong relationships.

(RCE) <u>Stuff in China is constantly changing.</u> "Rapidly Changing Environment" encapsulates the way things in China are changing more quickly than they are in most Western countries. This encompasses the economic, cultural and physical changes that have occurred, and continue to occur, as China develops. People who haven't been to China tend to discount the significance of ongoing changes there– after all, change isn't unique to China. Which is true. What IS unique, however, is the pace and scale. For example, hundreds of millions of China's urban middle-class citizens were penniless rural farmers 30 years ago. It took the US and Europe almost a hundred years to make that same change.

> **Some combination of these 12 elements explains most issues that Westerners face in business with Chinese counterparts.**

For instance, in trying to understand why a Chinese investor constantly reschedules meetings at the last minute, applying the model gives an explanation in terms of Long Term Orientation and Feudalism:

 The long term is what's most important

+

 Leadership equals lordship

= Chinese customers, investors and bosses are inconsiderate about wasting the time of others.

The Chinese have a fundamentally longer, more relaxed view of time than Westerners. Chinese people tend to view schedules as suggestions, rather than a fundamental organizing tools. As such, they are very often late and apt to change schedules at the last minute. Additionally, Chinese customers, investors and bosses all feel that they have the *right* to waste the time of their employees, investees and customers. They think this is inherent in their position in the relationship – they see themselves as being "higher" in the hierarchy and, therefore, entitled to do what they like. Thus, a Chinese investor wouldn't hesitate to keep you waiting or inconvenience you by rescheduling an appointment because she's not that concerned about time, and because she thinks there's nothing wrong with inconveniencing you anyway.

There are a huge number of possible combinations of these various elements, but the objective isn't for you to learn every permutation of the model. The objective is to help you make sense of the various cultural issues *behind* the behavior you're seeing. The objective is to give you a framework for understanding new situations as they arise and the ability to react in the most constructive way.

Of course, no model can reduce something as complex as a whole culture to a few short statements, or explain complicated interactions by stringing those statements together. Which is to say, this model is wrong. But it's also very useful.

Section II

Problems With People To Whom You're SELLING

Chinese Customers, Investors and Bosses

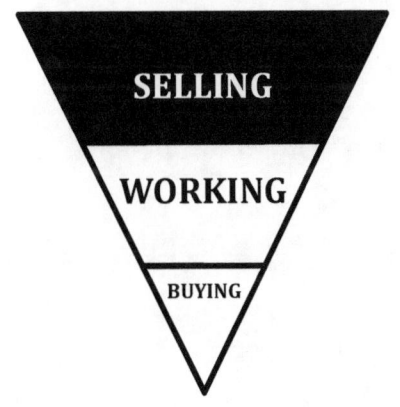

Customers, Investors and Bosses

"There is only one boss: the customer."

Walmart CEO Sam Walton

Increasingly, businesspeople in Western countries have Chinese customers, Chinese investors and Chinese bosses. This is the inevitable result of China's growing wealth and economic development. As Chinese companies invest abroad, they exercise greater control over the firms in which they've invested. As Chinese consumers acquire more disposable income, they become customers for Western firms with stuff to sell them.

Which puts the shoe very much on the other foot for most Western businesspeople, who've always been in the dominant position of a buyer or manager when dealing with China.

This change in roles can lead to friction and strife for both sides. Most professionals from Europe and North America find the new situation not only uncomfortable but also confusing.

So, where do you start?

The defining issue in dealing with Chinese customers, investors and bosses is **feudalism**.

The Chinese, and indeed most Asian cultures, do not accept the idea that all people are created equal, or that there is some natural equality that exists among human relations. In fact, quite the opposite – the Chinese believe in the inherent *inequality* of human relations. To them, in every relationship and in every interaction, someone is always on top and someone is always on bottom, based on the relative power each person holds.

Geert Hofstede, the father of modern cross-cultural management theory, called this quality "power distance." Power distance is the degree to which a person with less power or status accepts the authority of someone with more power or status. Most English-speaking countries score low on their power distance measurements – they generally believe that all people are equal. The Chinese, on the other hand, score very high on their view of power distance – they believe that people are not equal. To them, all relationships are defined by this inequality. This is the very essence of feudalism – a power structure where everyone agrees that people of higher status have more rights than people of lower status.

Confucius codified this thinking in The Five Relationships:

- King and subject
- Father and son
- Husband and wife
- Older brother and younger brother
- Senior friend and junior friend

In each case, the "higher" ranking party has the responsibility to guide and care for the "lower" ranking party; the "lower" ranking party has the responsibility to respect and follow the "higher" ranking party.

As foreign as this idea may seem to you, it is deeply ingrained in the thinking of your Chinese customer, investor and boss, and it will significantly influence the way they interact with you.

On the positive side, this way of thinking absolves you of a lot of personal responsibility, and it tends to be very, very durable –

once a Chinese person has formed such a relationship, they are likely to stay in it for a long time.

On the negative side, it makes many Westerners feel stifled, micromanaged, and disrespected.

In any event, it's an important aspect of Chinese culture that will have a big impact on your daily interactions with your Chinese customer, investor, or boss.

This section looks at these relationships with people to whom you are selling something – your products, your company, your time. They're your customer, your investor or your boss. They believe they have power over you and they don't hesitate to exercise that power. I'll discuss problems that you're likely to run into with these people and suggest constructive ways of addressing those issues.

Problem # 1 – Wanting The World

Handling Unreasonable Demands

 Leadership equals lordship

 All relationships are hierarchical and, thus, unequal

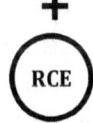 Stuff in China is constantly changing

= Chinese customers, investors and bosses are prone to making unreasonable demands.

What It's Like

Chinese customers, investor and bosses are like high-maintenance celebrities – they're used to getting their way, they feel like they're above everyone else and they live in a world where it's in their interest to be unreasonable.

The Problem

Chinese customers, investors and bosses tend to make a lot of demands that, to a Westerner, appear unreasonable. Partially, this is because Chinese customers and bosses *can* – the hierarchical and feudal nature of business relationships in China make it acceptable for superiors to express unrealistic wishes about the goals and performance of their subordinates. To some extent, this is also because so many things in China have changed so fast over the past 35 years that Chinese businesspeople have become accustomed to the idea that incredible things can be accomplished with hard work and the right motivation. One of my Chinese acquaintances grew up as a shoeless peasant in rural Sichuan and today is a Mercedes-driving millionaire. As a manager he regularly asks for things that seem impossible because, in his view, he's accomplished so much by attempting "impossible" things that he believes it's always worth trying.

This matters to you because:

1. Your Chinese customer WILL make unreasonable demands of you - there is virtually nothing you can do to stop this from happening or circumvent it,
2. Your Chinese customer doesn't care that he or she is inconveniencing you – he's accustomed to inconveniencing everybody,
3. You have to be ready to handle unreasonable requests with patience and decorum, and
4. You should consider that what they ask for MIGHT be doable, that it might lead to something better.

A Story

Right before Spring Festival, the most important holiday in China, Robert and his whole management team were summoned to their Chinese boss' office to explain why they had not implemented an idea that the Chinese CEO had proposed two years before. The idea was one of hundreds the CEO had proposed and there had been no indication that he placed any particular importance on that particular issue. Nonetheless, the CEO demanded to know why it hadn't been implemented and the Chinese boss demanded the same of Robert and his team. The Chinese boss insisted that Robert keep his whole department at work during Spring Festival to find a way to fulfill the CEO's demand. To Robert, this sounded totally unreasonable – people in the department had made commitments to far away family members, bought train and plane tickets, spent money on gifts for friends back home. To Robert, this seemed exactly like an employer in the US or Australia cancelling people's Christmas holiday on December 23.

Strategies – What You Can Do About It

Unreasonable demands are a common occurrence when you have a Chinese customer, investor or boss. Given that you can't avoid these demands, you CAN do the following:

1. Do NOT get angry, frustrated or emotional. That will not help you and, in fact, it will only make things worse.
2. Always say yes and smile. Say some version of yes that you can live with – e.g. yes I'll try to do that.
3. Realize they don't mean the requests literally. Contrary to the way a Western boss gives instructions, a Chinese boss doesn't literally mean that you should do exactly as he says.

In this context, it is more like a suggestion, or a statement of what the boss wants, rather than an actual order.
4. <u>Play your own game.</u> Pick the thing you want to do, the part of what the customer or boss said that makes sense, and do that.

Solution In Action

None of Robert's Chinese managers objected to the Chinese boss' demands and, on the contrary, they all agreed that they'd do as he asked and get the department working on the CEO's request immediately. When the management team left the Chinese boss' office, they told Robert that this request – having people work over Spring Festival – was impossible and there was no way of fulfilling it. Instead, one of the management team members organized a show of working on the problem, sending out self-serving email updates throughout the holiday. The CEO and the Chinese boss were happy with this outcome and praised Robert and his team for their dedication.

Problem # 2 – Being Treated Like A Child

Dealing With Condescension And Criticism

 Leadership equals lordship

+

 All relationships are hierarchical and, thus, unequal

+

 Face (perception) is more important than facts (reality)

= By Western standards, Chinese superiors can be condescending, repetitive and abrasive when giving criticism.

What It's Like

It's like being treated as if you were a wayward child.

The Problem

A frequent complaint about Chinese customers, investors and bosses is that they are condescending and unfairly critical of the people below them. This is a direct reflection of the feudal nature of such relationships in China – the boss believes they have the right, and even the responsibility, to criticize their underlings and lecture them on better ways of doing things. This can seem especially surprising when coming from a partner or peer, but the way a Chinese person sees it, if they are criticizing you it is because they have a higher position in the hierarchy (if only temporarily) than you do. This typically infuriates Westerners, who feel insulted by this kind of treatment. For Westerners, the impression is one of being treated like a wayward and not-too-bright child. However, the Chinese themselves don't see it in that way at all; in fact, my Chinese friends often see this as evidence that the boss cares about them and wants them to do better.

This matters to you because:

1. The natural Western reaction of getting angry about this treatment is counterproductive and
2. You're probably getting something out of the relationship (sales, investment, local expertise, your salary) that is worth preserving, which makes it in your interest to find a way to deal with this challenge.

A Story

A customer of mine in Xi'an, someone who had referred significant opportunities to me in the past, got angry about the fact that I hadn't coordinated one of my trips to China with him. I hadn't done that because, in my Western view, we didn't have any pressing business together at that time and I hadn't wanted to bother him. I called him at the last minute just to say that I was in town and invited him to come for a friendly drink with me. When he arrived, he was furious because in his mind my visits to China were a resource to be used to further our mutual business goals. Hence, by not calling him I'd wasted one of HIS resources. I was forced to sit and endure 3 hours of lecturing about the fact that I'd wasted this opportunity, as well as a list of critiques about what I was doing wrong in our effort to build some joint business in China.

While I fully accepted the premise of my Chinese customer's criticisms, I was furious at having to listen to him rehearse my mistake over and over again, interspersed with anecdotes about how much better he was at handling these cross-cultural, international interactions than I was.

Strategies – What You Can Do About It

This kind of lecture is pretty common when a Chinese person is delivering criticism. Given that you can't avoid your Chinese boss or investor making unreasonable criticisms, you CAN do the following:

1. <u>Don't get mad.</u> Getting mad or frustrated won't help. Making an angry statement, or otherwise showing your displeasure, REALLY won't help.

2. <u>Think of what you're gaining out of the relationship.</u> Ask yourself whether that's worth the price of being talked to in an uncomfortable way.
3. <u>Understand that your Chinese counterpart doesn't mean to be offensive.</u> This may seem incredible, but they were raised with a different cultural expectation.

Solution In Action

As I sat there, listening to my Chinese client berate me and getting furious about the way he was treating me, I tried to keep two things in mind: (1) he wasn't trying to be abrasive; in fact, by his lights he was being helpful, patient and understanding and (2) getting mad and storming out would merely have assuaged my ego at the cost of wrecking a profitable and useful business relationship.

Every Chinese person I told this story to thought the Chinese customer's behavior was completely common and in no way noteworthy. Virtually every one of them said it was evidence that the customer really cared about our business relationship and wanted it to succeed. Many of them related similar stories about dealing with their parents.

Problem # 3 – Drinking To Excess

The Ordeal Of Drinking Sessions

 Relationships are more important than rules

+

 China has a HUGE number of people in it

+

 The group is more important than the individual

= Business dinners with a lot of drinking are an important part of establishing trust for Chinese business people.

What It's Like

It's like truth serum.

The Problem

The Chinese are well known for drinking heavily at business dinners. In fact, a large percentage of my most successful friends in China have gout, despite only being in their 30s or 40s. One of the key risk factors for gout is the consumption of alcohol and rich foods.

The pervasiveness of heavy drinking at Chinese business dinners is mostly driven by a desire to understand what you're really like, what you're really thinking. The Chinese feel that drinking is an important part of building relationships, and one that gets around some of the limitations imposed by considerations of face and the habit of employing mostly indirect modes of communication.

This practice has increased as China's work force has become more mobile. This mobility means that virtually everyone shows up at their place of work with no ties to the community or the local group. The paucity of Chinese last names makes this problem worse because it means that it's easy for dishonest people to disappear into the crowd. (The top 100 names in China account for almost 80% of the population; the surname Li, alone, accounts for 100 million people.) All of which increases the desire of Chinese businesspeople to know who they're dealing with.

This matters to you because:

1. Participation in these drinking sessions is both more of an expectation, and carries more of a benefit, than in Western environments and
2. You need to have a plan for how you'll conduct yourself, as many practices that are normal in the West (e.g. politely saying you've had enough) are not acceptable in China.

A Story

Joseph was invited to a dinner with a Chinese government official to whom he'd submitted a bid for a regional project. When Joseph arrived at the Chinese official's office, that official's boss was on hand and, having never before met a foreigner, decided to come to dinner as well. The whole group went to the restaurant and throughout the course of the evening the various department members toasted Joseph and the Chinese official's boss. They also toasted Joseph's assistant, a young woman who'd helped the government departments in a number of ways. The toasting and drinking went on until the assistant started throwing up, at which time everyone got up to go home. Everyone was extremely happy with the outcome of the evening. They cheerfully cleaned up the young assistant and then took both Joseph and his assistant back to their respective hotels. Joseph's Chinese partner, who was on hand for the event, said it was about the most successful such meeting he'd ever attended.

Strategies – What You Can Do About It

Given that you can't wholly avoid drinking sessions with your customer, investor or boss, you CAN do the following:

1. Go along with it. To the extent possible, go along with the drinking. It may be hateful, but it's helpful.
2. Make an acceptable excuse. Religion, health issues (e.g. a cold) and driving are seen as acceptable excuses for not drinking, although they still leave your Chinese hosts wishing you HAD drunk with them. It would be considered extremely embarrassing and face-losing to mention alcohol-

ism as the reason you don't want to drink. Fitness (i.e. the idea that drinking too much is generally bad for you) or a general preference not to drink would be accepted, but would be judged in a slightly negative way, as "wimping out."

3. <u>Eat! Eat!</u> Food is usually served at the time of drinking and you should take advantage of that, eating to help offset the alcohol to some extent.
4. <u>Raise your glass anyway.</u> If you are not drinking, or have stopped drinking for the evening, you can continue to toast with juice or tea, and you should out of politeness.

Solution In Action

When he realized that the Chinese government official's boss was attending the dinner, Joseph knew that it would be a night of heavy drinking. He considered telling his hosts that he was taking antibiotics, as a way of excusing himself. However, Joseph realized that while the government official would accept that excuse, both he and his boss would be disappointed and it would count against him. Instead, Joseph decided to go along with the program and drink with the official and his boss. He ate when he could, good naturedly pulled the Chinese themselves into the drinking games when possible, and drank all the tea that was offered him. Although the evening went as badly as he'd feared from a drinking standpoint, it went extremely well in terms of improving his relationship with the Chinese government officials.

What was important to the Chinese clients was that Joseph was willing to drink and even to get drunk, to speak freely throughout, and to show that he had nothing to hide. Alcohol was an important part of the equation for them.

Problem # 4 – Not Our Expertise

The Push For Vendors To Provide All-In-One Solutions

 Don't let perfect be the enemy of good enough

 Relationships are more important than rules

 Stuff in China is constantly changing

=	The Chinese prefer all-in-one solutions.

What It's Like

It's like a Swiss Army Knife - the Chinese would rather have that than a box full of tools.

The Problem

Chinese customers want you to do a lot of stuff that Western ones don't. In particular, Chinese customers frequently want you to deal with an entire problem set, not just a particular part of it. They prefer all-in-one solutions, rather than piecemeal specialization. So, in addition to constructing the building itself, a construction company would be expected to deal with the planning commission, legal issues, engineering, landscaping, and infrastructure. They might also be asked to help the investors find and visit the site ahead of time, negotiate the land purchase, get visas for the investors and help the investors move country.

Partially, this is out of pragmatism – given the generally low levels of experience and professional development in China, choosing one solution to cover an entire class of problems is just easier. Partially, this is because things depend on relationship in China, so giving a wide range of responsibilities to one firm with whom you already have a relationship makes sense. Finally, the fact that things are changing so fast in China means that Chinese executives feel that it doesn't pay to learn about non-core issues – it's more efficient to let someone else handle those non-core issues.

This matters to you because:

1. It will help if you're prepared for these wide-ranging requests and have some way to respond favorably and
2. You may feel the need to identify a partner ahead of time, someone who can help you meet the requests from your Chinese or customer.

A Story

The first prospective client I approached in China was the CEO of a medical devices company. I knew that he wanted to expand his company overseas and I was pitching my services as a consultant. He was interested, asked me a number of relevant questions about different potential markets, and then asked if I could also help him buy a house in the US. Perplexed, I said I guessed that I could. He then asked if I could help him get a visa, if I could write the contracts for his overseas business, and if I could act as his local salesperson in the foreign market. I said that I could not, that I didn't have any knowledge or experience in those areas, that I was afraid I'd serve him badly if I agreed to do those tasks but that I'd happily assist him in finding firms with the appropriate expertise to help him. Instead of hiring me, he used a lawyer in the US, a Chinese immigrant who'd said yes to all of his requests. To me it was "obvious" that he'd chosen a significantly inferior service provider, but his view was that he'd chosen an all-in-one solution that would be good enough.

Strategies – What You Can Do About It

Although there's no way you can avoid getting these broad and seemingly unrelated requests from your customers, you CAN do the following:

1. Be prepared. You're going to get asked for a bunch of things you don't usually make or do, so try to imagine what those requests are likely to be and have a plan for how you're going to respond to them.
2. Be flexible. Just because you haven't done it before, doesn't mean you can't do it now.

3. <u>Partner up.</u> You don't have to do all the work yourself, although you may have to coordinate everything. Find appropriate vendors to support you and subcontract out the things you're not proficient at.

Solution In Action

Virtually every Chinese CEO I approached had similar requests, wanting a wide range of services, many of which had little to do with my core service offering. The successful approach I developed involved anticipating potential requests, never saying no (no matter how outlandish the request) and finding partners and subcontractors who could help me deliver the desired suite of services.

Problem # 5 – Being All Things

The Expectation That Every Employee Can Do It All

 Relationships are more important than rules

+

 Don't let perfect be the enemy of good enough

+

 Stuff in China is constantly changing

=	The Chinese expect people working for them to undertake a wide range of tasks, often unrelated to their professional training and experience.

What It's Like

It's like drinking wine from a coffee cup – it may not be the perfect solution, but if a coffee cup is what you have to hand, it's convenient and workable.

The Problem

In the same way that Chinese customers want vendors to provide a wide range of services, Chinese bosses want the people working for them to undertake a wide range of tasks. This is mostly just a function of pragmatism – for the past 35 years, China hasn't had a developed ecosystem of highly trained specialists, so the choice was between using the smart-but-inexperienced employee at hand, or doing nothing. Mostly, the inexperienced employees were able to do a job that was good enough to keep businesses running and growing. This has created an expectation among Chinese bosses that their employees are eager to try new things. The rapidly changing environment in China has provided fertile ground for this relationship-based way of working – as new skills were required, bosses appointed known, trusted employees to learn these new skills, which helped the business to grow, thereby requiring another set of new skills. The boss got richer and the employee continually gained valuable new skills, with concomitant increases in salary.

For Westerners coming from a system largely built around narrow professions and widespread specialization, the requirement to do things outside their field of expertise can seem bizarre and stressful.

The problem this gives most foreigners is that their Chinese boss or investor is likely to ask them to do things for which they have no professional training or experience.

This matters to you because:

1. It will help if you're prepared for these wide-ranging requests and have some way to respond favorably and

2. You may feel the need to identify a mentor ahead of time, or otherwise find a way to get comfortable about doing something in which you don't have a lot of experience.

A Story

A common situation for Westerners who go to work in China is that they assume that they're being hired for their specialized knowledge and experience, but when they start to work they find this is not at all the case. The Westerners think their highest value to a Chinese company is related to their specialized skills. Instead, they're tasked with many roles that have nothing to do with their experience and training. The Chinese company's theory is that because the Westerner had done well in their specialty, they'll also do well in these new things, and bring new ideas to the process.

Strategies – What You Can Do About It

Although there's no way to stop your boss from asking you to do lots of things you don't have any experience doing, you CAN do the following:

1. <u>Double down.</u> Although the Chinese are not as attracted to being specialists themselves, they respect the knowledge and experience of specialists and value their services. You can try to stick to your specialty, although this is a high-risk strategy and one that requires that you have something unique to offer.
2. <u>Explain your value.</u> Many Chinese bosses and customers don't understand the benefits of using a specialist and, thus,

believe the job can be done by someone who has more general skills. This means that if you want them to use you as a specialist, it's important to explain the value of a specialist's work.
3. <u>Give it a go.</u> The easiest thing to do is to give them what they want and just try your best at whatever they ask you to do. Although that strategy may seem inefficient to you, your Chinese customer, investor or boss is ready to pay that price, to have a less efficient solution from someone they know than a more efficient one from someone they don't.

Solution In Action

I see this pattern repeated every time I work with a Chinese company, and not just with foreigners. Employees are often simply moved into jobs because that's where the company needs someone at the moment. It's common to see engineers acting as HR directors, accountants working in sales, and lawyers acting as IT managers.

The most successful employees within Chinese companies are those employees who are willing to try something new, those people who don't mind starting over again in terms of learning a new role.

Problem # 6 – Bad Deals

Managing Bad Deals And Resistance To Paying

 Stuff in China is constantly changing

 Relationships are more important than rules

 The Cultural Revolution had a massive impact on Chinese society

= The Chinese often force bad deals on partners early on in the relationship, or resist paying for things (especially services).

What It's Like

It's like lawyers fees for a personal injury case – you want the expert (the lawyer) to prove his worth by winning the case before you pay.

The Problem

A problem that's very common for Western firms with Chinese clients is that they get asked to accept bad deals, and then the Chinese client still resists paying. This is particularly true for service companies.

A few things are going on here. First, the fact that China is still comparatively early in its economic development means that the value of complex goods and of most services is often poorly understood. This can be a problem because, as someone once said, a confused mind doesn't buy. The bad deal is a test of sorts for the partner, both in terms of loyalty and quality, and an attempt to shift the risk associated with paying for something they don't truly understand.

Resistance to paying for services is an attempt to shift performance risk to the vendor – the Chinese partner reasons that if the consultant (or lawyer or marketer or engineer) really knows what they're talking about, they should be willing to back it up by deferring payment until the advertised outcome is achieved. To some extent, it's like personal injury lawyers in the West – because the law is complex, most clients don't really know if they have a good chance of winning their case or not, so the model they prefer is one where the lawyer gets paid when and if they get a judgment in their favor. In this way the expert (the lawyer) bears the risk of delivering what he says is the benefit of using his services.

This situation is exacerbated by the fact that the vendor and the customer often don't have a prior relationship. A Western firm might rely on accepted business practice and the market reputation of the vendor, but a Chinese company is likely to want a personal relationship instead. The absence of a relationship makes it much easier for the Chinese company to justify forcing bad terms on the vendor, or not paying them.

This matters to you because:

1. It will impact your revenue model – if you're relying on the same level of acceptance of hourly rates from a Chinese client as from a Western one, you're likely to face challenges and
2. It will impact the risk profile of your business – you will almost certainly have to take a bad deal to start with, and then build your relationship from there.

A Story

When an English friend of mine first started trying to sell consulting services to Chinese clients, every one of the first 20 he approached resisted the idea of paying anything for the service he was offering. He spent months chasing small, low-paying deals, wondering whether it was worth being in the Chinese market at all. The central problem, he found, was that people didn't understand what he was selling and they didn't trust that he would deliver anything valuable to them. As his Chinese partner explained, "They want the foreign expertise you have to sell, and they think that you're probably very qualified and knowledgeable. But they don't know you, and they don't really understand the things you're talking about, so they're afraid that somehow you'll cheat them and they'll lose face."

Strategies – What You Can Do About It

Although there's no way you can avoid these tendencies in Chinese customers, you CAN do the following:

1. Try to use performance-based business models. Do what you can to align your interests with those of your client. Try to make it so that you get paid when they get what they want.
2. Offer them something they can easily understand. For instance, instead of consulting, offer to them a training course with a detailed agenda, supporting materials and a certificate of completion. This provides them a basis for establishing a relationship with you.
3. Keep the long term in mind. It's tough to get Chinese customers to trust you, but if you can, they are likely to stick with you for a long time.

Solution In Action

The approach that worked was to shorten the gap between the Chinese clients getting what they wanted (e.g. sales from external markets or identification of an overseas investment target) and him getting paid. The other thing that helped was to package his service as training or education – that is something the Chinese understand and can put a value on.

Problem # 7 – Saying Yes

The Expectation Of Subservience

 All relationships are hierarchical and, thus, unequal

 Face (perception) is more important than fact (reality)

= Chinese customers, investors and bosses don't like to be contradicted or challenged; they expect subservience.

What It's Like

It's like someone making a presentation in front of a group of people – the last thing they want is someone in the audience challenging or contradicting them.

The Problem

Something that strikes almost every Westerner who deals with groups of Chinese businesspeople is the extent to which the group defers to the opinion of the boss. You can usually tell who's in charge of a group of Chinese businesspeople, because it's either the person who's doing most of the talking, or it's the person at whom everyone keeps looking when they venture an opinion.

Chinese bosses do not encourage the kind of open discussion and respectful challenges that are common in Western business settings. They expect deference and they expect not to be contradicted when they speak. Openly challenging a Chinese boss is absolutely unacceptable, even in private; in public it would be considered totally disrespectful and insubordinate.

This matters to you because:

1. You need to keep yourself from contradicting or challenging your Chinese superior if at all possible,
2. If you DO contradict or challenge a Chinese superior, you're likely to offend them and have significant long term relationship problems from it. In their mind, you would have caused them to lose face, which is a terrible hurdle to overcome once it's happened and
3. You're probably getting something valuable out of your relationship with your Chinese customer, investor or boss that makes it worthwhile to come up with a way of dealing with this aspect of Chinese business culture.

A Story

Jonathan, a Westerner working for a Chinese state owned enterprise, struggled with the fact that his Chinese boss never listened to the suggestions he made during the boss' staff meetings, despite Jonathan's significant experience and industry knowledge. More than that, Jonathan could tell that his suggestions were irritating his Chinese boss, who frequently cut him off or brusquely moved the discussion along to another topic when Jonathan was making a comment. This distressed Jonathan in a number of ways, not least because the company was talking about doing things Jonathan knew had been tried, and failed, in other companies. Jonathan frequently spoke out against such ideas, and tried to bring facts into the discussion to demonstrate the need to reconsider the moves being contemplated. None of this had any effect and, if anything, the situation between Jonathan and his boss got worse.

Strategies – What You Can Do About It

Although there's no way you can avoid situations where you want to speak out against something suggested by your Chinese customer, investor, or boss, you CAN do the following:

1. Be careful in public. Do NOT contradict or publicly challenge a Chinese superior (e.g. a customer or boss). This will absolutely not help you and is likely to make the situation worse.
2. Say it softly. Couch any contradictions in the softest, politest, most round-about way possible. For instance, "Boss, that's an excellent idea. We should think of how to avoid the problems that XYZ Competitor had when they tried to launch this kind of product." This will save the face of the superior being challenged.
3. Think laterally. Try to think of a way to address the situation other than making your customer, investor or boss climb down from a position they've taken and thereby lose face.

Solution In Action

Jonathan noticed that one of his Chinese colleagues, someone with whom he was very close, was very much in the Chinese boss' favor, and was listened to carefully when he spoke. After talking to his Chinese friend, Jonathan started using an approach that turned out to be much more successful. First, he never openly disagreed with his boss – whatever the boss said, Jonathan would express agreement with. To the extent Jonathan did have concerns, he volunteered the information as if that were part of the implementation process; "That's a great idea, boss, that will really help. When we did that at my previous company, we had to spend a lot of time working with the IT guys to make it work efficiently." Second, he was conscious of NEVER putting his boss in the position of having to say that he was wrong. This worked much better than his previous approach and his relationship with the Chinese boss improved steadily after that.

Problem # 8 – Being Mistreated

Handling Disrespectful Behavior

 Face (perception) is more important than facts (reality)

 All relationships are hierarchical and, thus, unequal

= Chinese people are unconcerned about offending people below them.

What It's Like

It's like an old-fashioned queen or king – they don't care what the commoners think or feel, because the commoners' opinions don't matter.

The Problem

Chinese customers, investors and bosses often say things to their subordinates that Westerners view as highly insulting. For instance, I have many times witnessed bosses publicly say that one of their employees was wrong, that their performance was bad, or that they were stupid. This is because face is hierarchical and there's no obligation on the senior party to defer to, or even consider, the subordinate's feelings. Equally, Chinese subordinates see this as normal behavior by the boss and, while unpleasant, nothing special or worth getting too upset about.

This matters to you because:

1. If you're in a lower position versus a Chinese counterpart (e.g. if they are your customer or boss), you need to be prepared for the fact that they may treat you in a very patronizing and (to Western sensibilities) insulting way, simply as a matter of course,
2. Remember that it's important not to get mad or to openly show your displeasure, as that will likely make the situation much worse and
3. You need to plan on a response that is both acceptable to your Chinese superior and that you can live with.

A Story

June, a Chinese friend of mine, told me about an internal sales conference she'd attended where the CEO had addressed the assembled salespeople and then asked if there were any questions. A young man stood up and asked about the company's product development schedule and when certain things would be available for sale. The CEO calmly waited for the young man to finish his statement and then told the assembled group that his question was an example of their weakness as a sales organization, that if they were better salespeople they'd be focused on selling their current products instead of asking about new ones, and that the young man clearly didn't know what it took to be a salesman. June didn't feel that the CEO's comments were rude or out of place but, rather, that they showed his accessibility, strength of will, and focus as a leader.

Strategies – What You Can Do About It

Although there's no way you can stop Chinese customers, investors or bosses from discounting you or treating you disrespectfully, you CAN do the following:

1. Realize it isn't personal. When you're in a subordinate position, and on the receiving end of rude behavior, understand that you're not being singled out, that's how the customer, investor or boss always acts,
2. Do NOT get angry about it. Nothing good will come from expressing your anger at being talked to in a way you find insulting. Your customer, investor or boss thinks they have that right and will see YOU as the unreasonable, insubordinate, insulting one if you respond in an open and angry way,
3. Think of a response you can live with. For example, "I'll try to do better next time," and
4. Play the game. Understand that accepting the patronizing behavior of your Chinese superior will get you further with them than not accepting it.

Solution In Action

The employees who are the most successful in a Chinese company NEVER get angry or upset about the "abuse" they receive from their superiors. Likewise, the most successful Chinese salespeople are the ones that accept ANY comment their customer makes with a smile and a promise to do better in the future.

Problem # 9 – Being Closely Watched

Dealing With Being Micromanaged

 Leadership equals lordship

 All relationships are hierarchical and, thus, unequal

= Chinese bosses are micromanagers.

What It's Like

It's like a kindergarten teacher – they give the kids very specific tasks and manage them closely throughout the assignment.

The Problem

Chinese bosses look over your shoulder, tell you how to do things, and require you to get permission for small things in a way that takes micromanagement to a new level. For many Chinese executives, this is a reflection of the fact that they started out working in factories where the low skills of their workforce and the strict requirements of their foreign buyers made quality control a nightmare. For many, the only solution was detailed oversight of everything that every worker did. Many have carried that philosophy into the office, as well. The larger reason is that the feudal nature of Chinese organizations means that bosses are paternalistic and actually see it as their duty to supervise even small details of their subordinate's work.

This matters to you because:

1. If you have a Chinese boss or client, you need to be mentally prepared to be micromanaged and
2. You need to plan ahead for how you're going to react to this micromanagement, to develop a strategy for responding appropriately.

A Story

Helen, a Chinese friend of mine who had worked in the US for many years returned to China and joined a large company there. Helen was utterly dismayed by the way that her Chinese boss required everyone to seek his direct approval for everything they did, by his focus on small details, by the way he pointed people in contradictory directions, by the way he yelled at people for not understanding his instructions, and by the fact that he didn't listen to anyone else's opinions or suggestions. The Chinese boss simply believed that being a micromanager and a martinet was the correct way of getting things done. Even more to Helen's dismay, most of the managers in her company were this way to some extent.

Helen struggled at first with what felt like a demotion – in the US she'd had significant freedom over her time, her team and her budget. In China, however, she felt as though she were being treated like she had no experience or business sense. However, she observed that EVERYONE around her was being treated the same way. She also understood that her boss was intimidated by her US experience, which often made him act defensively towards her.

Strategies – What You Can Do About It

Although there's no way you can stop your Chinese boss from micromanaging you, you CAN do the following:

1. Don't get upset. If you have a Chinese boss, don't get upset when they micromanage you. It's not personal, it's just how they do things.
2. Remember to be respectful and subordinate. An aggressive, disrespectful tone or behavior will cause you other problems in dealing with the boss.
3. Make a show of effort. Your Chinese boss, investor or customer wants to see a lot of effort on their behalf. It makes them feel that they're not somehow being cheated, that you're dedicated to them.

Solution In Action

Helen adopted a consciously respectful and subordinate tone in every conversation she had with her boss, and she started to inform him of EVERYTHING she did. Any time the boss asked the team to do something, Helen loudly took the lead in coordinating everyone's efforts. While this was contrary to her nature and experience, it paid off in that both her boss, and her boss' boss, soon started delegating responsibilities and authority to her. As she explained to me, once her boss saw that she wasn't resisting his efforts to closely manage her work, he became bored with following up with her all the time. Because she made it easy for him to know what she was doing, and because she was eager to help, he soon started giving her more responsibilities.

Problem # 10 – Constant Effort

The Preference For Effort Instead Of Efficiency

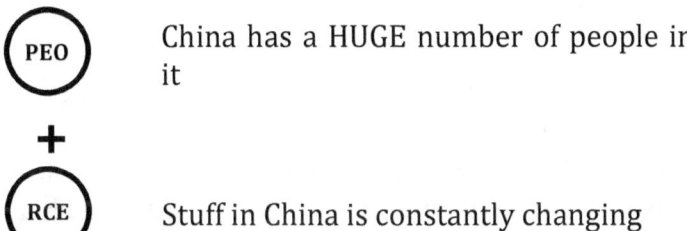

(PEO)	China has a HUGE number of people in it
+	
(RCE)	Stuff in China is constantly changing
=	The Chinese value effort more than efficiency.

What It's Like

It's a little bit like Nike's motto – just do it. Don't worry about technique or scheduling or talent, just do it.

The Problem

China has huge numbers of increasingly skilled workers and efficiency just doesn't matter very much to them. The huge number of people and the rapid pace of economic development in China over the past 40 years, combined with the low state of education and experience, has meant that it has been in people's interest just to do things as best they could, without reference to efficiency. Every *minute* between 1980 and 2014, 20 workers moved from the farm to an industrial or professional job in the cities of China. This incredible surplus of labor has made efficiency a very low priority for the Chinese.

This matters to you because:

1. It's a bad idea to try and compete with the Chinese on anything that relies on brute effort,
2. Solutions based on greater efficiency don't have the same resonance for Chinese managers as for Western ones and
3. The focus on effort means that Chinese customers and bosses like to see outward signs of hard work.

A Story

Paul, an Australian friend of mine who works for a Chinese company in Beijing, made a study of the company's work efficiency that showed that the Chinese company needed half the employees it had, representing a potential savings of several billion US dollars. While the report was widely circulated and regarded as intellectually interesting, only one Chinese executive saw it as actionable information. The other executives simply were not impressed with the idea that things could be done more efficiently.

In discussing the report with some of the Chinese executives, Paul said, "Wouldn't it be better if we worked smarter, not harder?" One of the executives replied, "No, it would be better if we worked harder AND smarter." The Chinese executive didn't see any contradiction between those two ideas.

Strategies – What You Can Do About It

Although there's no way you can circumvent the Chinese emphasis on effort over efficiency, you CAN do the following:

>Pay attention to face time. Your Chinese customer, investor or boss wants to see you making a big effort. In addition to actually DOING the work, it's important to be SEEN to be doing the work.

1. Do NOT try to compete with the Chinese on effort (or time). You cannot win that game, they will always work longer than you will. Try to think of another way to distinguish yourself by, for instance, being a source of "global best practices."
2. Realize that the Chinese aren't impressed by efficiency. A common complaint from Westerners is that the Chinese work long hours because they are inefficient; a common complaint from Chinese people is that Westerners go home early because they are lazy. Both groups get the job done, but getting the job done isn't the only important factor. For the Chinese, doing something in a more efficient way isn't always a persuasive reason for doing it that way. In fact, Chinese people can view efficiency as an excuse for laziness, a bigger sin in their eyes.

Solution In Action

Paul told me that the reception his report got, and the subsequent conversations he had with the Chinese management, profoundly impacted his view of what the company wanted. He never again made a proposal based solely on the idea that it was more efficient. Instead, he set himself up as an authority on best practices and talked about making things "easier" (which had a personal appeal to the people adopting the change) and higher quality. He also said that he made a bigger effort to demonstrate the hours he was putting in.

While many other Westerners have left the Chinese company, he's been with the company for years and has steadily risen in their ranks.

Problem # 11 – Ignored Suggestions

Getting Them To Accept Your Ideas

  Leadership equals lordship

 Step-by-step improvement is better than revolutionary change

 The long term is what's important

= To get a Chinese customer, investor or boss to accept your idea, it usually needs to be an incremental improvement that they think they have suggested themselves.

What It's Like

It's like the roles that husbands and wives used to assume, whereby the husband appeared (even to himself) to be in control, but was actually doing what the wife wanted him to do.

The Problem

Chinese customers, investors and bosses often don't care about YOUR idea for how to solve a particular problem, they simply want you to make THEIR idea work. This flies in the face of management theory as practiced in the West, where bosses tend to care less about HOW something gets done (assuming it gets done in a legal and ethical way) and more about the final result. Because Chinese bosses have an opinion about how things get done, it's usually harder to get them to accept an idea that they, themselves, didn't come up with. They also bring a significant prejudice in favor of incremental improvements as opposed to revolutionary changes. This prejudice is deep-seated and applies to many different aspects of Chinese life.

The combination of these cultural prejudices, along with an orientation towards the long term, make Chinese bosses reluctant to accept ideas that aren't theirs, especially if the idea puts forth a significant change to an accepted process. As a practical matter, this means that to get your idea accepted, you usually have to make the Chinese boss think the idea is somehow theirs, and that it represents an incremental improvement over the existing way of working.

This matters to you because it determines whether or not you get things accomplished that will keep your customer, investor or bosses satisfied with your product or performance.

A Story

A number of my Western friends and colleagues in China work for large international consulting firms. Many have been working at the same Chinese client for years, and so have had ample time to understand their company cultures. Most of them have worked internationally for many years, and have exposure to companies in a number of countries. Almost to a person, they all say that one of the things they can be sure of is that their ideas and suggestions are unlikely to be implemented. While this is not, in itself, unusual (lots of clients pay for advice that they don't follow), the thing that surprises them is the scale on which this happens with Chinese clients. Most of them were hard pressed to come up with any example of a Chinese client actually implementing one of their ideas.

Which begs the question, "What were the Chinese companies paying for?" Mostly the Chinese companies paid for implementation help – they had a goal and a solution and they just wanted the consultants to make that solution work.

Strategies – What You Can Do About It

Although it's always a challenge to get your Chinese boss to accept your suggestions, you CAN do the following:

1. <u>Make it their idea.</u> Find ways to parrot their suggestions back to them, but with a twist that allows you to accomplish what you want. If you cannot, try to break it down into several stages, such that each one gets you closer to your goal.
2. <u>Make it small.</u> Make it seem like a natural, evolutionary change from the current situation. The Chinese tend to pre-

fer incremental changes over revolutionary ones, so present your idea in that light.
3. <u>Give them the whole picture.</u> When proposing a step-by-step solution (the preferred way of working for Chinese people) be prepared to describe the process through to the end, as well as the impacts the changes will have. Giving Chinese people the whole picture gives them a feeling of comfort that you really understand the problem, the solution, and the impacts from both.

Solution In Action

The Western consultants who are the most successful in selling services to Chinese clients are the ones that propose a big project that's based on something they've heard from the Chinese person in charge of the project, and that will make that person look good. The project is usually far-reaching in scope, but broken down into small pieces, each one of which delivers some advantage of its own. For instance, a large-scale IT system transformation that can be staged such that each improvement yields a tangible and visible benefit.

Problem # 12 – Underlying Meanings

Understanding Indirect Communications

 Face (perception) is more important than facts (reality)

+

 Things are better when everyone gets along

+

 Relationships are more important than rules

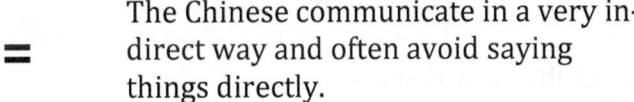

= The Chinese communicate in a very indirect way and often avoid saying things directly.

Note: A discussion related to indirect communications also appears in Problem # 20 and Problem # 28

What It's Like

It's like discussing something a friend may be sensitive about (their weight, the fact that they're balding, their age, problems their children are having) - you often talk around the subject, but don't refer to it directly, out of deference to their feelings.

The Problem

The Chinese communicate in a much more indirect way that Westerners, saying things in a soft, often euphemistic way, that allows everyone involved to preserve face, no matter what the outcome of the discussion. This is important in a group-oriented society where the underlying expectation is that at the end of the day, everyone will have to get along and tolerate each other enough to move forward together.

This matters to you because:

1. It's important to be sensitive about potential face issues when talking to a Chinese person,
2. It's important to interpret what a Chinese person is saying in light of the context and
3. Because it's often just as important to consider what's not said as what is said. In general, this is an area that's fraught with challenges and misunderstandings.

A Story

There's an old joke in China about two friends, an American named Mike and his Chinese friend Du, whose car is broken.

"Mike, do you need anything from the grocery store? I'm going and I'm happy to pick up whatever you need," the Chinese friend says.

"No, I'm good, thanks," Mike answers.

Du thinks for a moment.

"You know, it's going to be very hot today."

"Yes, I'd heard that," Mike answers.

Du thinks for another moment.

"You know, if you ever need anything, I'm always happy to help."

"Yes," Mike smiles, "I know. Thanks."

Daring greatly, Du tries one more time.

"You know, it's a long way to walk to the store."

Finally Mike gets it. "Du, would you like a lift?"

The next day, Du's car is fixed, but Mike's won't start.

"Du, my car car is broken," Mike says. "Could you give me a lift to the store?"

Strategies – What You Can Do About It

When dealing with Chinese and their indirect way of communicating, you CAN do the following:

1. Consider the context. When Chinese people are speaking to you, consider the possible meanings of what they're saying, and weigh that in the context of what you know.
2. Beware false positives. Know that Chinese people will rarely tell you anything negative or unpleasant in a direct way –

it embarrasses them. They may agree with you even if they think that what you're saying is completely wrong.
3. <u>They think you know what they're talking about.</u> Know that Chinese people think you understand this indirect way of speaking – they think you know what they mean, when often you don't.

Solution In Action

Of all the people I know, the foreigner who best understood the Chinese way of speaking indirectly was an Australian named Michael. Michael spoke no Mandarin and had no particular knowledge about or connection with China, but he fundamentally understood the concept that Chinese communication was less about what was being said and more about the *context* of what was being said. So, for instance, when he was asked why a Chinese boss had cancelled a project that the boss had previously said was a good idea, Michael would ask, "When he said it was a good idea, was that just an easy way of making you feel good? Was there any OTHER reason why it was in his interest to say the project was a good one? What about when he cancelled it? Was it just after he met with HIS boss? Was it after a budget meeting? Was it after someone had complained about some aspect of the project?" He was relentless about trying to understand the context, and he understood that no one would tell him negative things to his face, so he had to collect external clues in order to piece things together.

Problem # 13 – Lack Of Clarity

Coping With Vague Communications

 Face (perception) is more important than facts (reality)

+

 Leadership equals lordship

+

 All relationships are hierarchical and, thus, unequal

 = The Chinese customers, investors and bosses protect their face by being vague.

What It's Like

It's like parents giving vague explanations when their children ask questions the parents don't know the answer to – "you'll understand when you get older" or "because that's the way it is."

The Problem

Chinese people expect leaders (bosses, parents, CEOs, managers) to be vague in their instructions and vague about their intentions. The underlying reason for this is that it allows the leader to take credit for things that go well ("that worked because the underlings correctly interpreted my instructions") and a way to assign blame if things go badly ("that didn't work because the underlings screwed up the execution of my excellent plan").

This matters to you because:

1. You need to know you won't get clear instructions from a Chinese in a higher position than you and you'll have to act on your own,
2. You need to know that part of your job as a subordinate is to accept the blame for things that go wrong and
3. It's a mistake to try and pin a Chinese superior down on their meaning, because they consider that face-losing.

A Story

Once, during an executive meeting I attended at the Chinese company where I worked, we were discussing the meaning of a corporate directive that the CEO had issued and its impact on a project we were running. I innocently asked if we couldn't just ask the CEO for clarification. The other executives looked at me as if I were both stupid and incredibly rude. It was later explained to me that no, we could not ask the CEO what he meant, that it was part of our job to figure out what he meant.

This pattern repeated itself almost every time an executive of any stature issued an order or directive – it was vague and the subordinates spent a huge amount of time trying to decide what was meant.

Strategies – What You Can Do About It

When dealing with a Chinese customer, investor or boss and the fact that they are being vague, you CAN do the following:

1. Know you're not going crazy. If you think a Chinese person in a senior position sounds vague, it's because they ARE being vague.
2. Live with it. Mostly, a junior person cannot hope to get clarity from a senior person in China, because that would expose the senior person to the risk of losing face.
3. Take a guess. The best thing to do is to make your best guess about what the leader meant and do whatever is most likely to succeed and allow the leader to claim that his instructions were responsible for the project's success.
4. Don't ask for clarity. It is rude to try and pin down a senior Chinese person on their meaning or intention.
5. It's unfair, but it's part of the job. It's important to remember that part of your job as a vendor or subordinate is to accept blame and shield the customer or boss from a loss of face when something goes wrong, which is the ultimate purpose of these vague communications.

Solution In Action

Once I understood that the CEO was TRYING to be vague, I quite enjoyed reading his announcements and trying to guess what he meant. I simply accepted that neither I nor anyone else knew what he meant and, therefore, it was best to take a guess and act on that.

Problem # 14 – Proving Yourself

Dealing With The Search For Loyalty

 Relationships are more important than rules.

+

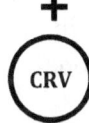 The Cultural Revolution had a massive impact on Chinese society

+

 Leadership equals lordship

= The Chinese value loyalty very highly.

What It's Like

It's like the mafia – the environment is dangerous and dependent on relationships more than rules, so personal loyalty is extremely valuable.

The Problem

The Chinese have a preoccupation with personal loyalty. This is a logical extension of their reliance on guanxi, instead of rules, to regulate the behavior of people in society – if there are no rules, then loyalty is the only way to be sure that someone will treat you in a positive way. The Cultural Revolution took this reliance on personal relationships to a new level. In addition to undermining the basis of existing laws, the Cultural Revolution brutally tested people's personal relationships by setting targets for arrests and encouraging people to inform on one another. This created an environment where distrust was high and personal loyalty was at an absolute premium.

The other issue at play is the feudal nature of work relationships in China. Customers and bosses feel that they have every right to demand proofs of personal loyalty from their subordinates.

This matters to you because:

1. It's important to consider loyalties when proposing a solution to a Chinese customer, investor or boss,
2. You need to keep in mind the fact that your Chinese customer, investor or boss will constantly and relentlessly look for you to demonstrate your personal loyalty to them and
3. Loyalty will often trump all other considerations when a Chinese person is making a decision.

A Story

Gina, a Swedish friend of mine working for a Chinese company, told the story of an incredibly smart and capable executive who continually protected and promoted a tremendously foolish and incompetent manager. When Gina asked about this, and tried to understand why the executive continued to support the incompetent manager in spite of all his failures, and the availability of much better managers, Gina was told that the incompetent manager's loyalty to the executive was longstanding and absolute and, because of that, the executive would prefer to keep him around, no matter how badly he performed.

Strategies – What You Can Do About It

When dealing with a Chinese customer, investor or boss, and the fact that they highly value loyalty, you CAN do the following:

1. Get the lay of the land. Don't expect a Chinese person to make a decision that goes against someone who is a loyal ally of theirs (e.g. a longstanding friend or a family member). Neither efficiency, nor effectiveness, nor better service, nor higher quality, nor lower price trumps loyalty in the mind of a Chinese person.
2. Know it takes time. Understand that, as a foreigner, it may take you a LONG time to demonstrate your loyalty to a Chinese superior.
3. Realize that those ties bind. Know that once you have established your loyalty to a Chinese person, that bond will likely endure for a long time and in the face of many difficulties and failures.

Solution In Action

Gina told me that she'd been so impressed – and appalled – by the example of the incompetent Chinese manager and the power of loyalty in a Chinese organization that she reevaluated her whole approach to working within the company. She mapped out on a whiteboard the significant decision-makers above her in the department, as well as what she understood about their supporters and detractors. She said the process gave her a good idea about the main "alliances" within the department, and a very clear picture about how her boss would interpret her actions in relation to others. She understood that her boss would probably have a similar view of loyalty as the other Chinese executive had and, as such, she needed to consciously try and build that perception in her boss' mind. She said it made her life vastly easier to understand what mattered in the organization, and to have a way to maximize that.

Problem # 15 – Being Suspect

Coping With The Lack Of Trust

Relationships are more important than rules

+

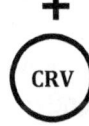
The Cultural Revolution had a massive impact on Chinese society

+

All relationships are hierarchical and, thus, unequal

= The Chinese tend to think that people cannot be trusted.

Note: A discussion about trust also appears in Problem # 23.

What It's Like

It's like someone who's been through a bad breakup and thinks that everyone of the opposite sex is untrustworthy.

The Problem

As discussed in the previous chapter about loyalty, and for many of the same reasons, the Chinese tend to think that people cannot be trusted. This was one of the things that struck me most powerfully when I first started working in a Chinese company – it was clear that people didn't trust me very much. I didn't feel insulted, merely perplexed – why would they hire a financial executive they didn't trust? The nature of the job is that you have access to all the company's dirty laundry and the bank accounts! What I came to understand, however, is that it wasn't personal, or specific to me in any way – ALL newcomers were viewed with suspicion. My Chinese friends would frequently say, "It's easy for a foreigner to be respected but it's hard for them to be trusted."

This matters to you because:

1. This effect is more pronounced with other Chinese than with Westerners (who are seen as coming from a rules-based culture and, therefore, more likely to treat everyone equally), providing you a small advantage and
2. It generally means that standards of proof are higher in China than in the West.

A Story

Many large Chinese companies require EVERY employee below the board level, from the janitor to VPs, to clock in and out of work. There is absolutely no trust that, unless people are sitting in the office being supervised by their manager, that they will be working on behalf of the company. This contrasts strongly with companies in Europe and North America, which often have flexible time or working from home arrangements.

Strategies – What You Can Do About It

When dealing with a Chinese customer, investor or boss and their lack of trust, you CAN do the following:

1. <u>Don't get frustrated.</u> It's not personal.
2. <u>Realize that trust takes time.</u> The best antidote for being unknown is to become known, through maintaining personal relationships.
3. <u>Being a foreigner helps.</u> Understand that the Chinese tend to be less suspicious of foreigners they don't know than of Chinese they don't know. They believe that Westerners come from a cultural background that predisposes them to acting according to the rules, whereas Chinese people don't come from such a background. This can be an important advantage when doing business with the Chinese.
4. <u>Do them a favor.</u> The most powerful way of building trust, aside from investing years in developing the relationship with your Chinese counterpart, is to do them a favor. Even better is to do a favor for their child. Help them get into an overseas school, write them a recommendation, refer them to a job, help with a visa – anything that is easier for you to do than for them to do themselves. This isn't easy – it takes a certain amount of trust even to know enough to do such favors. But it works like a charm.

Solution In Action

The most successful strategy I ever used to build trust with a Chinese executive was something I fell into by accident. A Chinese executive who sat down the hall from me one day asked if I could help his son, who was about to graduate from university in the US. The son was looking for a job and needed help. I agreed, and over the next few weeks I helped the son rewrite his resume, register on job search websites, and prepare for interviews. In the end, the son didn't find a job in the US and returned to China to work. However, the Chinese executive was so touched that I'd taken such pains over his son that he's gone out of his way to be helpful, and to vouch for me with other Chinese executives and businesspeople, ever since.

Problem # 16 – Friends & Family

Dealing With Favoritism And Nepotism

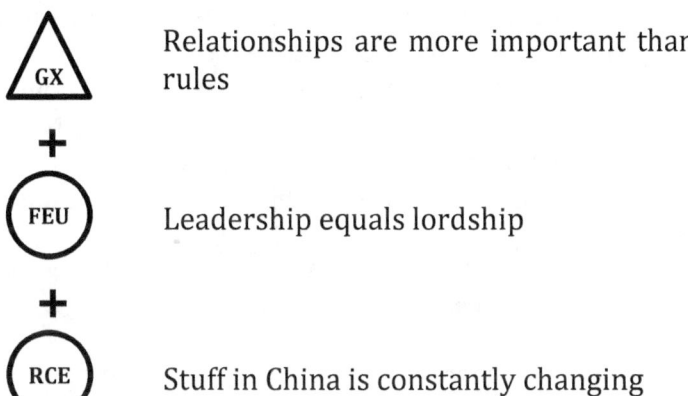

= The Chinese are far more accepting of favoritism and nepotism than Western people are.

What It's Like

It's like a rich kid getting into a top-notch university because his mother donated a building – many Western people see that at wrong and unfair, but most Chinese would feel that it's only natural that a child should benefit from the money and influence of his parents.

The Problem

The dominance of guanxi as a guiding principal in Chinese society means that favoritism and nepotism are far more common, and far more widely accepted, in China than in North American or European cultures. In fact, whereas both of those concepts are seen as negative and even illegitimate in the context of Western business, until very recently they were actually seen as positive in China, because they are strong evidence that the patron showing such favoritism was being loyal to his family and friends.

This matters to you because:

1. Offerings that ignore this fact are likely to struggle for acceptance among the Chinese and
2. In any situation with such a dynamic at play, it will always either work for you or against you, it will never be irrelevant.

A Story

One of China's richest people is Wang Jianlin, who's the CEO of Dalian Wanda, a Chinese conglomerate. Dalian Wanda's operations extend across a variety of industries and continents, and market watchers have openly speculated about whether his son, Wang Sicong, would take over the $100 billion empire once the 61 year-old Wang Jianlin retires. Following a string of minor scandals wherein the son made a number of boorish, arrogant statements about his status as the scion of the vastly wealthy Wang family, the father ruled Wang Sicong out as a possible successor, saying he didn't have the maturity or character to lead the firm. However, soon after, the elder Wang established an investment fund for his son to run. This was widely interpreted as a way for the younger Wang to prove himself and get back into his father's good graces. Now, after a string of moderate successes, that seems to be happening – Wang Sicong appears to be back on track to take over his father's business empire.

The equivalent in the West would be if Paris Hilton were tapped to take over Hilton Hotels – she's shown no great genius for business, and has nothing like the education or experience of any number of executives already working in the company. Her sole qualification is her name. So it is with Wang Sicong and Dalian Wanda.

While this would seem outrageous in the West, in China almost everyone accepts that this is just how things work.

Strategies – What You Can Do About It

If your Chinese customer, investor or boss employees a personal favorite or family member, you CAN do the following:

1. <u>Understand the lay of the land.</u> Always strive to understand who favors whom and who is related to whom in a Chinese organization, because these relationships have a huge impact on how decisions are made.
2. <u>You're either for them or against them.</u> Either you're on the side of someone with a powerful sponsor or you're against them, there is no middle ground. So pick a side and get on it.

3. <u>Blood is thicker than water.</u> Remember that favoritism and nepotism will usually trump other considerations like competence or efficiency. That being the case, try to think of a way of getting what you want without competing with the person being favored. Even better, think of a way to align yourself with the favored person and help them get what they want. That will earn you a powerful ally.

Solution In Action

After having worked as a consultant at an electronics company in Shanghai, Ted, an American, joined them as a VP in their operations department. Something he'd noticed during his time as a consultant was that every Westerner who came and worked in the department was eventually sidelined, or they simply left. He further observed a significant difference in the attitude of Chinese and Western employees to the COO, who was the CEO's son. The Chinese employees were deferential to the point of being obsequious, whereas the Westerners were much cooler towards him. Ted knew this was because they didn't think the son was particularly qualified for his position.

When he joined the company, Ted made a conscious decision to assiduously support the CEO's son. He actively looked for opportunities to do things that reflected well on the COO. This strategy turned out well, and Ted has found himself increasingly supported in his own career within the company.

Problem # 17 – Time Wasting

Understanding The Chinese View Of Time

 The long term is what's important

What It's Like

It's like the difference between the way a teenager and a middle-aged person view time. Teenagers have a view that's immediate and dramatic, whereas middle-aged people have a longer, more tempered view of time.

The Problem

A strongly held cultural belief in China is that the long term matters more than the short term, which affects many aspects of getting things accomplished in China.

When the renowned cultural anthropologist Geert Hofstede first measured the Chinese orientation towards time, their score was literally off the chart: Hofstede's scale went from 0 to 100 (a larger score representing a longer term view of time) and the Chinese averaged a score of 120. He subsequently adjusted the scale to accommodate the new data, but China's score remained far higher than that of others he'd surveyed.

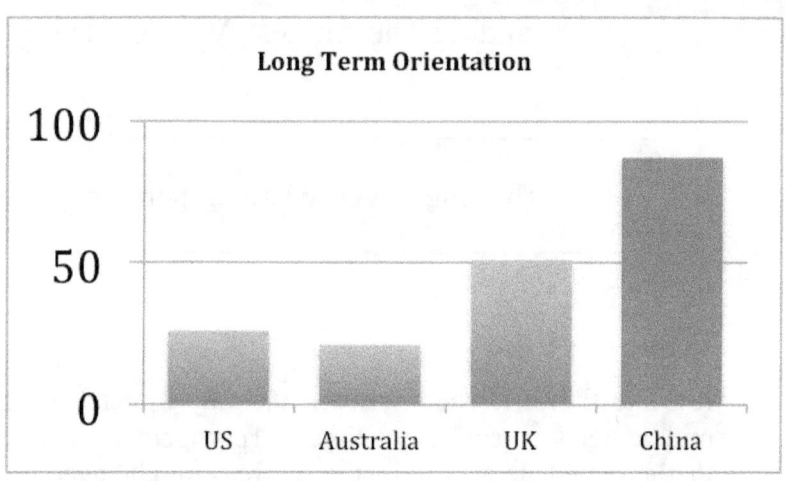

This matters to you because:

1. Virtually everything you want to do in China, from holding meetings to launching new product offerings, will take longer than you expect,
2. Chinese people tend to have a much more relaxed view of schedules than you do, so tightly scheduling things is a strategy that's likely to fail, and
3. Chinese business people generally don't put the same premium on time efficiency as you do.

A Story

While visiting a provincial city in China, a government official accompanied me to provide introductions to two local firms that had shown an interest in my firm's services. I'd scheduled four hours for the trip and let the government official know that I had a dinner meeting with a client that evening. The first meeting went as scheduled and we even finished a few minutes early. Seizing the opportunity, the official said that there was another company, a local investment incubator, which he'd like to stop by "on the way" and introduce us to.

We went to the investment incubator, whose management received us warmly and gave us a presentation about the technology park they operated. They then asked if they could introduce us to some of their investee companies. I said that nothing would give me more pleasure, but that we had a prior engagement at another company in town. The government official said, "No problem," got on his phone and rescheduled the meeting with the second company. Delighted, the management of the investment incubator began calling companies into their conference room.

Dozens of people showed up, none of them with any idea why they'd been called. I gave my spiel about our firm and what we do and started to answer questions from the group. More people came in, lost because they hadn't heard my introduction. So I gave the introduction again. The first group of people were bored and pulled out their phones. Then another group of people came in. The whole meeting dissolved into chaos. Although I tried several times to call the government official's attention to the fact that we needed to go to the second meeting, he was delighted with the energy of the meeting we were having.

Strategies – What You Can Do About It

While you can't change the way your Chinese customer, investor or boss views time, you CAN do the following:

1. Be patient. No one likes to exercise patience but, believe me, when dealing with time issues related to the Chinese you will need all the patience you can muster.
2. Plan for long time frames. Don't be surprised that things take longer than you expected.
3. Relax. Do NOT set up plans with the Chinese that rely on tight, exact timing, or high levels of time efficiency (i.e. build time for delays into your plan).
4. If the last minute didn't come, nothing would get done. Understand that the Chinese are absolute magicians when it comes to getting stuff done at the last minute. Look at the Beijing Olympics.

Solution In Action

Although I was unable to keep the Chinese government official to our original timetable, I was able to accept what was going on and take a longer view about it. The connection with the government official was a useful one for me to make, and nothing good would have happened if I'd insisted on moving along when he clearly wanted us to spend time at the investment incubator. Having experience this kind of thing before, I'd left significant "cushions" in my schedule for the day. I'd warned the client that I was to have dinner with that I was going to be out in the countryside and might be late; he thought the idea of a foreigner going out to the Chinese countryside fascinating and hilarious, so he was quite happy to delay the dinner if needed. In the end, everything worked out, mostly because I had anticipated delays and I hadn't tightly scheduled my appointments.

94

Section III

Problems With People With Whom You're WORKING
Chinese Peers and Partners

Peers & Partners

"Succeeding in business is all about making connections."

Virgin CEO Sir Richard Branson

The issue that constantly comes up when people talk about their Chinese business partners is the feeling (or certain knowledge) that they're being cheated.

Which is why the defining issue in dealing with Chinese peers and partners is *guanxi* **(relationships)**.

Chinese culture is built around an emphasis on the group, which means that group dynamics are central to their way of thinking. The reason that *guanxi* is such a big thing with the Chinese is that it's what guides people's behaviors. The Chinese don't rely on rules or professionalism to nearly the same degree as people from the West. Instead, they rely on personal relationships.

The Cultural Revolution took this reliance on personal relationships to a new level. In addition to undermining the basis of existing laws, the Cultural Revolution brutally tested people's personal relationships by setting targets for arrests and encouraging people to inform on one another. This created an environment where distrust was high and personal loyalty was at an absolute premium.

Although the memories of that time fade with each new generation, people in China are still significantly impacted by the lessons of the Cultural Revolution. Which is why personal loyalty is much more important in business dealings in China than in the West.

The key thing to remember when dealing with Chinese peers and partners is that their commercial behavior is dominated by their personal loyalties. The reason you're so likely to get cheated by a Chinese partner is not that they're inherently less honest than you are, it's that within their framework of personal loyalties, there's nothing wrong with swindling a stranger who lives far away. Equally, to the extent that you HAVE earned their personal loyalty, you'll be the *beneficiary* of those same calculations.

Unfortunately, because loyalty takes time to establish, it's usually hard to have that kind of relationship with your Chinese peers and partners. They're likely to have such relationships with others, mostly with other Chinese people. While you and I think professionalism ought to be enough, the Chinese want something deeper and more personal.

This section looks at relationships with people with whom you work. They're your peers and partners. I'll discuss problems that you're likely to run into with these people and suggest constructive ways of addressing those issues.

Problem # 18 – Being Cheated

Dealing With Dishonest Partners

 Relationships are more important than rules

+

 Be pragmatic – don't let perfect be the enemy of good enough

---

= The Chinese often try to go around their partners – they try to cheat them.

What It's Like

It's like Napster – people found a way to get music without going to the record store; they found a way to cut out the middleman.

The Problem

Being cheated by a Chinese partner is almost proverbial. Even among the Chinese themselves this cultural tendency is well recognized. This cheating generally takes three forms: (1) money-related cheating where a Chinese partner takes payment and then fails to deliver the agreed upon product or service, or vice versa, where the Chinese partner refuses to pay for something already delivered, (2) customer-related cheating where the Chinese partner works to cut you out of whatever deal you have by going directly to your customer and (3) technology-related cheating where the Chinese partner reverse engineers your product or process and then offers their own version for a lower price. This problem is tied up with the *guanxi*-based culture in China, and with pragmatism – if you can gain an advantage by cheating someone you're not particularly close with, why not do it?

This matters to you because:

1. You need to be on the lookout for situations where your Chinese partner is trying to go around you, or otherwise cheat you,
2. You need to take whatever precautions are practicable to prevent them from cheating you. For example, make sure you're providing something that cannot easily be duplicated, like a secret process, and
3. You should plan for the fact that they ARE going to cheat you and have a backup plan. The most effective backup plan is another partner.

A Story

An industrial supply business in the US developed a new market by repurposing a ceramic product they sourced from China for use in the US oil & gas business. For two or three years, things went extremely well and the company was highly profitable. Executives from the US company repeatedly traveled to China to work with their supplier in order to improve the product. These improvements were unique and promised to deliver significant profits to the company. Then, quite suddenly, problems emerged in the relationship with the Chinese supplier. At almost the same time, the US company's customers all started reporting that they'd found a cheaper source. To no one's surprise, the new source turned out to be the Chinese supplier.

Strategies – What You Can Do About It

While you can't stop your Chinese partners from trying to go around you, you CAN do the following:

1. <u>Stay alert</u>. Always be cognizant of the potential for your Chinese counterpart to go around you. Think of some way to keep this from happening – keeping your contacts secret, binding your other contacts legally, or make sure there is a hard financial reason why it's better for the Chinese to act with you than to go around you.
2. <u>Cozy up</u>. The Chinese have a saying: "First business friendship, then business." (先做朋友后做生意 xiān zuò péngyǒu, hòu zuò shēngyì). Work to form a longer-term relationship with your Chinese counterpart, as this will help ensure that you are treated more favorably.
3. <u>Do that jujitsu thing</u>. Work to create a situation in which your Chinese counterpart can't act in a way that hurts you without also hurting himself. If possible, make him beholden to you, or exposed to you, in some other way. For instance, if you were to help the child of your Chinese colleague to get a job, or get admission into

university, they would be far less likely to do something that was counter to your interests.

Solution In Action

Jason, a Chinese friend of mine living in the US, set up a business selling wine to a distributor in China. He took a number of steps to make sure that it would be difficult for his Chinese partner to go around him. First, he used his own network of connections to find a partner in China, someone he could trust at least somewhat. Second, he spent a lot of time getting to know the partner, and forming a relationship with him. Finally, he made sure the export license was in HIS name and that the suppliers were known only to HIM, and not to his partner in China. Thus, he created a situation where it wasn't easy for his Chinese partner to go around him.

Problem # 19 – Finding Fault

Navigating The Blame Game

 Perception (face) is more important than reality (facts)

+

 All relationships are hierarchical and, thus, unequal

+

 Relationships are more important than rules

= The Chinese are very concerned about assigning blame.

What It's Like

It's like people who have had a minor car accident in a car park – someone must be blamed and both sides try to make sure it's not them.

The Problem

Chinese people are very interested in who's to blame for any perceived failure that occurs. While this is true in all cultures, it's much more evident in China than in the West. This is rooted in concerns about face and about status within the group. The importance of blame leads to a lot of scapegoating and blame-shifting behavior within Chinese organizations.

This matters to you because:

1. If you are working for a Chinese boss (or serving a Chinese client) it's part of your job to accept the blame when things go wrong,
2. When you are dealing with Chinese people in any circumstance, blame will be high on their agenda when things go badly and
3. The risk of being blamed is often a big inhibitor to getting Chinese people to do something new.

A Story

Wang was the general manager of an African subsidiary of a Chinese multinational. The Chinese head office was pressuring Wang to make a sale to a large African customer. The Chinese multinational's biggest competitor was also pursuing the same contract. Faced with losing market share to a competitor, Wang had to offer many concessions to the customer. The outcome was predictable – Wang's company won the contract, but with ruinous terms. In most Western firms, this would have been seen as a difficult but unavoidable situation – the multinational was faced with either losing market share to its biggest competitor, or accepting a bad deal. In the West, no one would particularly have been held to blame given the realities of competing for that contract.

In the Chinese multinational, however, this was not the view. Shortly after the bad contract was signed, Wang was recalled to China and demoted. Despite the extenuating circumstances, he alone was saddled with the blame for having signed the bad deal.

Strategies – What You Can Do About It

While you can't change the way your Chinese peers and partners play the blame game, you CAN do the following:

1. Avoid blame like the plague. While it may seem scheming and self-serving to you, it's critical to avoid blame as and when you can, especially when the blame is being directed at you by a peer or partner. If a customer, investor or boss blames you, you have to accept it, even if it's unfair, because that's part of your function as a vendor or subordinate. But if someone who's not your superior tries to shift blame to you, or include you in something blameworthy, you have to avoid it at all costs.
2. Try to get them to focus on the problem. Understand that Chinese people are often reluctant to take chances because they are afraid of being blamed for the outcome, much more so than in the West. Getting them to focus on the problem instead of the blame (e.g. "because we don't have time for worrying about blame right now, we have to salvage the situation with the customer") will help them be more constructive and take more chances.

Solution In Action

The people in Chinese organizations who are most effective at avoiding blame are those people who are closest to the person in charge. These people use their position to present every situation in a way that deflects blame onto others. This strategy doesn't make them loved among their peers, but it does work very well in terms of keeping them out of trouble.

Problem # 20 – Getting The Gist

Understanding Indirect Communications

 Face (perception) is more important than facts (reality)

+

 Things are better when everyone gets along

+

 Relationships are more important than rules

= The Chinese communicate in a very indirect way and often avoid saying things directly.

Note: A discussion of indirect communications also appears in Problem # 20 and Problem # 28.

What It's Like

It's like discussing something a friend may be sensitive about (their weight, the fact that they're balding, their age, problems their children are having) - you often talk around the subject, but don't refer to it directly, out of deference to their feelings.

The Problem

The Chinese communicate in a much more indirect way that Westerners, saying things in a soft, often euphemistic way, that allows everyone involved to preserve face, no matter what the outcome of the discussion. This is important in a group-oriented society where the underlying expectation is that at the end of the day, everyone will have to get along and tolerate each other enough to move forward together.

This matters to you because:

1. It's important to be sensitive about potential face issues when talking to a Chinese person,
2. It's important to interpret what a Chinese person is saying in light of the context and
3. Because it's often just as important to consider what's not said as what is said. In general, this is an area that's fraught with challenges and misunderstandings.

A Story

Early in my time working in China, I was called on to make a presentation on significant differences between the Chinese company and its Western counterparts. One discrepancy I'd noticed was in the way the IT systems worked. In discussing my presentation with one of my colleagues, he said that the difference I was pointing to was interesting, but didn't I agree that the current IT system was much better than the previous one? This confused me, since I'd never seen the previous system and, anyway, that seemed completely irrelevant to the question I'd been asked. I mentioned this to my secretary who explained that the implementation of the current IT system had been overseen by one of the executives, who would be insulted if I made any negative comparisons to it. My colleague had been trying to draw my attention to this fact by mentioning the previous IT system.

Strategies – What You Can Do About It

When dealing with Chinese and their indirect way of communicating, you CAN do the following:

1. Consider the context. When Chinese people are speaking to you, consider the possible meanings of what their saying, and weigh that in the context of what you know.
2. Beware false positives. Know that Chinese people will rarely tell you anything negative or unpleasant in a direct way – it embarrasses them.
3. They think you know what they're talking about. Know that Chinese people think you understand this indirect way of speaking – they think you know what they mean, when often you don't.

Solution In Action

Something that helped me recognize when Chinese people were trying to tell me something in an indirect way was to watch their body language. I came to understand that if they were telling me something innocuous, but looked worried, that it was probably worth me thinking harder about what they were NOT saying. I also developed the habit of NEVER accepting a positive comment at face value – until I could prove otherwise, I always assumed they were simply being polite.

Problem # 21 – Unshared Wisdom

Dealing With The Fact That Knowledge Is Power

(RCE)	Stuff in China is constantly changing
+	
(FEU)	Leadership equals lordship
+	
△ GX	Relationships are more important than rules
=	Chinese tend to treat knowledge as power.

What It's Like

It's like the new kid in school who often sets themselves up as an expert on something obscure. This knowledge gives them power in the absence of status or existing relationships.

The Problem

The degree to which Chinese organizations create internal divisions in order to hoard information is striking. In Chinese, these divisions are known as bùmén qiáng (部门墙) and they are pervasive. On a personal level, people horde information in the same way. In both cases they are treating knowledge as power and they are reluctant to share it.

The reasons for this tendency are complex. First, the fact that things are evolving so fast in China means that there's a considerable advantage to possessing relevant information. That information is likely to be harder to come by, and to become obsolete quicker, than in North America or Europe. Second, feudalism and guanxi dictate that information is shared on the basis of relationships, and on what serves the boss' interests. Thus, Chinese managers and executives are likely to hoard information and dole it out only when there's a direct and short-term benefit to them.

This matters to you because:

1. It means that, to some extent, YOU will need to view information in this way yourself, in order to maximize your authority within the organization and
2. You need to be aware of how others are protecting their information, to understand what's likely to be off limits, or at least difficult to get, for you.

A Story

Thomas, a French friend of mine, once proposed a change in the way his company did something to his Chinese boss. The suggestion was met with silence and Thomas later came to understand that the Chinese boss was actually irritated about it, because the proposal was something that the boss had already ruled out. Thomas also found out that one of his peers had been fully aware of the Chinese boss' attitude but had said nothing to Thomas. When Thomas asked one of his Chinese friends why the colleague hadn't warned him about the situation, the Chinese friend said, "Why would he tell you that? It didn't make any difference to him. In fact, it's probably better if you look foolish, because it makes him look smarter."

Strategies – What You Can Do About It

When struggling with the Chinese tendency to treat knowledge as power, you CAN do the following:

1. <u>Expect a closed book.</u> Expect delays in trying to get information out of Chinese people, as they will be reluctant to share it.
2. <u>Get others to help you.</u> Cultivate Chinese friends and colleagues who's interest it's in to help you understand and avoid mistakes. Lots of Chinese people are flattered to help a foreigner, especially if it doesn't interfere with their own goals.
3. <u>Align your goals.</u> When trying to get information, it's best to make it in their interest to give you the information you need. For example, will it somehow make them look good or powerful? Can they share in the credit for what you're doing? Will it help them avoid a problem of some kind?

Solution In Action

After being embarrassed in front of his Chinese boss, Thomas understood that he had to be careful about what he DIDN'T know. The expectation that his colleagues wouldn't tell him when he was making obvious mistakes led him to find Chinese friends who WOULD help him recognize when this was happening. This turned out to be very successful, and helped him avoid similar problems in the future.

Problem # 22 – Friends Like These

Adjusting To The Lack Of Team Spirit

 Face (perception) is more important than facts (reality)

+

 The Cultural Revolution had a massive impact on Chinese society

+

 Relationships are more important than rules

 Chinese people frequently lack the kind of team spirit that businesses in the West take for granted.

What It's Like

It's like a group of boys who are competing for the attention of a girl they all like – they may be civil to each other, but they will work to undermine each other in an effort to elevate their own status.

The Problem

By Western standards, Chinese groups frequently show a lack of collegial helpfulness and team spirit. This may seem strange, given the group orientation of Chinese culture but, in fact, it's an outgrowth of it. Chinese people are very concerned about their status within the group, which is expressed in terms of face. Face is always comparative, meaning that it's just as effective to make someone else lose face as it is for you to gain face. It may be too dangerous to actually *cause* someone to lose face (that's a guaranteed way of making an enemy), but *allowing* them to lose face by not helping them is much lower risk. *Guanxi* and the lessons of the Cultural Revolution intensify the process, because it pushes people to help only those group members who are very close to them. All of which leads to teams that are usually not as cohesive as one might imagine them to be.

This matters to you because if you approach relationships with peers, colleagues and partners with an expectation that they will treat you in a friendly and helpful way you are likely to find yourself de-positioned, undermined and disadvantaged in a number of subtle ways.

A Story

Nancy, a Chinese friend of mine who'd attended university in the US and then worked for 20 years at a US tech firm in Silicon Valley, returned to China to take an executive position at a Chinese tech company. Despite her qualifications and experience, she soon found herself isolated and ineffective; eventually she was demoted. When I asked her what had happened, Nancy explained that she'd simply failed to take into account that some of her peers saw her as a threat and that they had done an effective job of undermining her. While she'd dealt with rivalries in the US, she was unprepared for the intensity of competition among her Chinese peers, or the fact that the other executives saw the political maneuverings as legitimate.

Strategies – What You Can Do About It

When dealing with the lack of team spirit shown by your Chinese peers and colleagues, you CAN do the following:

1. Assume you're on your own. Unless you can identify a clear reason why someone should help you, it's safer to assume that they do NOT want to help you.
2. Beware Greeks bearing gifts. Your peers and colleagues are often not your friends and they think it's perfectly legitimate to do whatever they can to make you fail or look bad.
3. Don't throw the baby out. As in any culture, individuals are all different. Many Chinese colleagues WILL be helpful and team spirited, so don't judge everyone by a single standard.
4. Trust but verify. Don't jump straight into blindly trusting a Chinese colleague's professionalism or team-spiritedness. Instead, observe and judge them over time. They need to earn your trust before you give it to them.

Solution In Action

After being demoted, Nancy decided that the biggest change she needed to make was to understand that she was on her own and that her peers would be happy to see her fail. This gave her a more ruthless perspective on dealing with her peers, and led her to be much more cautious about who she trusted. Eventually this allowed her to progress within the company and regain the ground she'd lost.

Problem # 23 – Untrustworthy

Coping With The Lack Of Trust

 Relationships are more important than rules

+

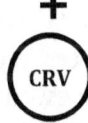 The Cultural Revolution had a massive impact on Chinese society

+

 All relationships are hierarchical and, thus, unequal

= The Chinese tend to think that people cannot be trusted.

Note: A discussion of trust also appears in Problem # 15.

What It's Like

It's like someone who's been through a bad breakup and thinks that everyone of the opposite sex is untrustworthy.

The Problem

As discussed in regard to loyalty, and for many of the same reasons, the Chinese tend to think that people cannot be trusted. This was one of the things that struck me most powerfully when I first started working in a Chinese company – it was clear that people didn't trust me very much. I didn't feel insulted, merely perplexed – why would they hire a financial executive they didn't trust? The nature of the job is that you have access to all the company's dirty laundry and the bank accounts! What I came to understand, however, is that it wasn't personal, or specific to me in any way – ALL newcomers were viewed with suspicion. My Chinese friends would frequently say, "It's easy for a foreigner to be respected but it's hard for them to be trusted."

This matters to you because:

1. This effect is more pronounced with other Chinese than with Westerners (who are seen as coming from a rules-based culture and, therefore, more likely to treat everyone equally), providing you a small advantage and
2. It generally means that standards of proof are higher in China than in the West.

A Story

Martin, an English marketing executive who came to work in a Chinese company, was surprised at the response he got when he sat down with the product development manager to talk about the marketing plan for a new offering.

"What's special about the new product? Why will anyone want to buy it?" Martin asked.

"It's unique in the market. None of our competitors has anything like it," the Chinese product development manager said.

"Great! What's unique about it?" Martin asked.

"I can't tell you," the Chinese product development manager answered.

"I don't understand," Martin said. "You can't tell me what's unique about the product? Why would anyone want to buy it?"

"Because it's the best thing on the market," the Chinese product manager said.

"But you can't tell me why?" Martin asked.

"No," the Chinese product manager said. "It's confidential."

"You mean we can't tell people what's special about the product?" Martin asked.

"Yes, we can't tell them. And I can't tell you. It's confidential," the Chinese product manager said.

"Why?" Martin asked.

"Because it's confidential," the Chinese product manager said.

The issue, as Martin found when he talked to his Chinese friends in the company, was that the Chinese product manager didn't know Martin and, therefore, wasn't willing to trust him, even though they both worked for the same company.

Strategies – What You Can Do About It

When dealing with a Chinese boss, customer or investor and their lack of trust, you CAN do the following:

1. <u>Don't get frustrated.</u> It's not personal.
2. <u>Realize that trust takes time.</u> The best antidote for being unknown is to become known, through maintaining personal relationships.
3. <u>Being a foreigner helps.</u> Understand that the Chinese tend to be less suspicious of foreigners they don't know than of Chinese they don't know. They believe that Westerners come from a cultural background that predisposes them to acting according to the rules, whereas Chinese people don't come from such a background. This can be an important advantage when doing business with the Chinese.

Solution In Action

Martin eventually enlisted the help of a Chinese colleague who was friendlier to him, and who had known the Chinese product manager for a long time. Using his Chinese colleague as a go-between and character reference, Martin was finally able to get the information he needed.

Problem # 24 – The Greasy Pole

Managing Shifting Power Dynamics

 All relationships are hierarchical and, thus, unequal

+

 The group is more important than the individual

+

 Relationships are more important than rules

= The Chinese are highly political and their group dynamics are constantly shifting.

What It's Like

It's like parliament or congress – everyone is constantly scrabbling for position and alliances are always shifting.

The Problem

The mechanics of hierarchy and the way group dynamics work within Chinese organizations push Chinese people to be VERY political. This extends into areas that can seem unreal to Westerners. For instance, I once came to understand that there was a political subtext to the number and placement of trees in the campus of the Chinese company where I worked – some executives thought they represented a genuine response to the Chinese government's push to improve environmental awareness, others thought it was just window-dressing, all of which was complicated by the fact that the tree supplier was the brother of one of the executives.

This matters because if you don't approach group interactions in a political way, you're likely to find yourself without power or authority in the group.

A Story

Acting as a member of the Finance Committee of the Board of Directors in a $50 billion Chinese technology company gave me a unique opportunity to observe the intensely political game that went on within the group. I observed that every interaction was a zero-sum game – there was always a winner and a loser, always someone who was going up and someone who was going down in the hierarchy. Even things as mundane as maintenance schedules had a political subtext. I later came to realize that virtually all Chinese organizations have this characteristic.

Strategies – What You Can Do About It

While you can't stop your Chinese colleagues from being highly political, you CAN do the following:

1. Play to win. You cannot be a spectator in a Chinese group – you are part of it and your power and authority are increasing or decreasing with every single action you take and every word you say. So play like it matters, because it does.
2. Consider context. The Chinese are massively contextual – where someone is from, who their spouse is, who they used to work for, what they had for lunch all matters. As a Westerner you cannot hope to master the subtleties involved, but at least try to be aware of the big issues at play.
3. Look up. The most important consideration in a Chinese organization is who your sponsor is. So don't worry about befriending the people at your level, concentrate on being useful to the people above you.
4. All's fair. It may be distasteful to you, but doing things purely for the political advantage it gains you – or the political disadvantage it saddles your peers with – is considered normal and rational in a Chinese group.

Solution In Action

By playing the most intensely political game I could, I was able to hold my own on the Finance Committee. The biggest thing I did was to choose two Chinese Finance Committee members as patrons and do everything I could to make them look good. I would prepare intensely for the meetings, thinking of information I could bring or arguments I could advance in the meeting that would reflect well on my patrons. Despite being the first and only non-Chinese person on the Finance Committee, by looking up and playing to win, I was able to navigate the shifting power dynamics.

Section IV

Problems With People From Whom You're BUYING
Chinese Employees, Subordinates & Vendors

Employees, Subordinates & Vendors

"We should always be disposed to believe that that which appears white is really black, if the hierarchy of the Church so decides."

Saint Ignatius

While no one can hold a candle to Chinese employees when it comes to working hard, Western managers are constantly dismayed by their inefficiency. Equally, North Americans and Europeans with Chinese vendors wonder what fresh hell awaits them when their next shipment comes in – things may be going splendidly, nothing may have changed on the Western side of the relationship, and then, suddenly, something inexplicably bad happens.

Why, you ask?

The defining issue in dealing with Chinese employees, subordinates and vendors is **hierarchy**.

Chinese subordinates spend a huge amount of time trying to guess what their bosses are thinking and what they want. At the same time, Chinese bosses encourage this by being paternalistic and vague. This creates a work environment where subordinates are reticent to voice their own opinions and, instead, spend a lot of time trying to figure out what the boss REALLY wants. It also makes things very inefficient.

This style is in stark contrast to prevailing Western management theory, which emphasizes efficiency through empowerment of employees and clarity of instruction.

This often presents Western managers with an unpalatable choice. In order to get exactly what they want from their Chinese employees they have to micromanage them, telling them to do things in a detailed way that can seem both off-putting and inefficient. On the other hand, if they empower their employees by allowing them to manage themselves, the Chinese employees often feel uncomfortable and unsupported, making them even more inefficient.

While Western managers usually think it's not their job to tell a subordinate HOW to do something, Chinese subordinates expect exactly this kind of instruction. You may see this as micromanagement, but they simply see it as management.

Keep hierarchy foremost in your mind when dealing with Chinese employees and vendors.

This section looks at relationships with people from whom you're buying something – mostly they're your employees and vendors. I'll discuss problems that you're likely to run into with these people and suggest constructive ways of addressing those issues.

Problem # 25 – Father Figures

The Need For A Directive Management Style

 All relationships are hierarchical and, thus, unequal

+

 Leadership equals lordship

= The Chinese expect to be micromanaged.

What It's Like

It's like small children at school – the kids need very specific tasks from the teacher and the teacher needs to check in on how the kids are doing very often or the kids get nervous.

The Problem

Because of the pervasiveness of paternalism in Chinese culture, Chinese subordinates actually want to be micromanaged. They find it comforting and familiar. To a large extent, this is because it's what they've grown up with, both personally and professionally.

This matters to you because if you have Chinese staff, you need to either micromanage them or specifically train them how to be more self-directed.

A Story

A Chinese friend of mine explained the process for implementing a project inside of the Chinese company where we worked. As a former executive in Western companies, I was used to being given free rein to achieve corporate goals according to my own way of thinking and management methods. My friend explained that in a Chinese company it didn't work like that. Even at the most senior levels, goals were assigned by superiors and then the subordinate checked back in at very short intervals to make sure they were performing according to the superior's idea. This involved the subordinate verifying, many times, that they were on the right track. To me, this seemed bizarre – even low level supervisors in the West worked on their own initiative, and no manager would ever be promoted to the executive level if they sought reassurance at each step of the process. But to the Chinese, that seems like the proper way.

Strategies – What You Can Do About It

While you can't stop your Chinese employees from preferring a micromanaging style, you CAN do the following:

1. <u>Be detailed.</u> If you have Chinese staff, you need to be clear with them on your expectations, especially if that expectation is that they will act on their own. This will need to be reinforced many times before it will be accepted. For example, tell them, "I'd like your suggestions on how best to do this. I'd like you to give me three options and tell me which one you think is the best."
2. <u>Be directive.</u> In most Western companies, a directive management style is seen as negative and the sign of a weak, even incompetent, manager. But the Chinese expect to be told, not asked, what to do. Not being directive confuses them and makes them nervous. For example, give them a specific task and tell them to come back and report their status the next day. The next day, repeat the process, such that you're effectively giving them daily guidance on what to do.

Solution In Action

Although it was completely against my nature and previous training, when I worked in a Chinese company, I adopted a much more directive and detailed style of management. The mainstay of this was giving my staff limited direction and making them come back to me on a daily or every-other-daily basis for further instructions. I found this style of management inefficient and tiresome, but it worked much better than a hands-off style, which left the staff feeling unsure about what to do, and which often led to me not getting the outcome I wanted from them.

Problem # 26 – Unchallenging

The Chinese Propensity To Always Say Yes

 All relationships are hierarchical and, thus, unequal

+

 The long term is what's most important

+

 Face (perception) is more important than facts (reality)

= Chinese people don't dare to challenge their boss, even when the boss is wrong – they always say yes.

What It's Like

It's like when your parents or grandparents are saying something you know is outdated or untrue, but you don't correct them out of respect for their age and position in the family.

The Problem

Chinese staff are very unlikely to challenge their boss, or even to express an opinion in a strong way without knowing ahead of time that their boss agrees with them. This is primarily driven by hierarchy, which drives Chinese people to focus on what the boss wants. One of the things I found hardest about managing my team in China was getting them to tell me what they really thought. "What do YOU think, CT," was the most common response. They were thinking of the long term (what if I remembered their unguarded comment in the future and held it against them?) and about how to avoid the embarrassment of giving the "wrong" answer. Generally speaking, Chinese subordinates will agree with whatever the boss says and will not challenge her.

This matters to you because:

1. It is a bad idea to challenge your Chinese customer, investor or boss and
2. It's important to realize why you're not getting challenged if you ARE the customer, investor or boss.

A Story

I attended a Chinese board meeting where the CEO began expounding an idea for a product that had been tried at several other companies and which had always failed due to a lack of market interest. He directed his attention to the head of R&D, with whom I'd previously discussed this exact topic, and the reasons behind the failure of this particular product line. To my astonishment, the head of R&D agreed warmly with the CEO's proposal, saying he was sure it would be a hit, that the company would steal a march on all its competitors by being first to market with this product. It subsequently transpired that the R&D executive reported that development of the CEO's idea was taking longer than expected, with the result that it was perpetually put off until an unspecified future date. But the head of R&D never told the CEO it couldn't be done – he simply said "yes".

Strategies – What You Can Do About It

While your Chinese subordinates will always want to defer to you and say yes, you CAN do the following:

1. Realize you're not getting the whole story. When your Chinese employees are agreeing with you, understand that they may only be doing it out of politeness and a sense of hierarchy.
2. Make allowances. Given that you're probably not getting the whole story, or a realistic view of whether your ideas are workable or not, make allowances in your planning for the fact that things may go quite differently than you think they will. If possible, find other ways to assess things, e.g. by asking disinterested parties what they think.
3. Emphasize blame-free thinking. One of the main reasons why your Chinese subordinates say "yes" all the time is because they're worried about what will happen if they say "no." If you want them to be more open with you, give you more honest opinions, and challenge you more, then you have to emphasize over and over that such behavior won't count against them, or make them subject to accusations of disloyalty or insubordination.
4. Couch it in terms they can understand. The most successful strategy for getting Chinese subordinates to act more openly

and to challenge you more freely is to couch it in terms of other cultural values, like face. For example, explain that if you propose something that YOUR boss (or customer or investor) won't like, that will cause YOU to lose face, and that part of their responsibility is to help make sure that doesn't happen. In that way, they're responding to your direct request (they feel comfortable being directed), and they relate your request to a sensitivity they share (face), which makes it easier to do something that usually feels uncomfortable to them (tell the boss she's wrong).

Solution In Action

In order to get my teams in China to challenge me and give me their honest opinions, I have to relentlessly emphasize the idea that I won't be angry with them if they disagree with me, and that by doing so they're helping me to not lose face in front of others. It usually takes more than a year to get them to accept this idea and to consistently act on it. One young woman in particular, someone who's worked with me for several years, now regularly tells me, "CT, I don't think you're right about that. I think we should do something different." While this sounds mild to a Western ear, it represents significant progress from the complete unwillingness to challenge me that she showed when we first started working together.

Problem # 27 – A Black Box

Managing The Fact That Your People Won't Tell You What's Really Happening

 The group is more important than the individual

+

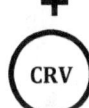 The Cultural Revolution had a massive impact on Chinese society

+

 Face (perception) is more important than facts (reality)

= Chinese subordinates won't give you an objective and complete description of situations they're involved in.

What It's Like

It's like someone recounting a story about an altercation – they're likely to tell the truth, but not the WHOLE truth; they'll leave out discreditable bits and things that complicate their position.

The Problem

A combination of guanxi (the fact that they don't have a close relationship with the boss), the general mistrust that's the legacy of the Cultural Revolution, and the importance of face (which makes Chinese people want to avoid being the bearer of unwanted news) drive Chinese subordinates to hold things back when they're answering questions or describing a situation to the boss. While this is true for people everywhere, it is much more pronounced in Chinese subordinates, who are greatly worried that they will be criticized or held responsible for something they say.

This matters to you because if you have Chinese subordinates it's imperative to understand that there are many things they are NOT telling you.

A Story

Matt was the American COO of a manufacturing plant in China. He told me a story about his company having run into problems with the Ministry of Commerce, because the company had violated export rules in handling some of their products. Essentially, the company had taken samples from their factory (which was located in a Free Trade Zone) to a lab (which was located outside the Free Trade Zone). The local Chinese inspector, who was well known to the factory personnel, had ruled these movements as illegal exports. When Matt asked his Chinese subordinates if they'd known that the local official would view things in this way, the Chinese subordinates said yes, they'd known that because the Chinese inspector acted the same way with other factories where they'd worked. When Matt asked why they hadn't warned him about this potential problem, the Chinese subordinates answered, "Because you didn't ask us."

Strategies – What You Can Do About It

While your Chinese subordinates will always tend to reveal less than you expect them to, you CAN do the following:

1. Be meticulous. Try to think of the details of how something will play out, or the factors in a situation that might possibly be important, and be sure you've asked the direct question.
2. Think like a lawyer. Try to think about what HASN'T been said or what's been assumed and ask questions related to these areas.
3. Prepare for things to go off the rails. Budget the time, capabilities and money needed to recover from unexpected problems because in China, much more than in the West, they are likely to happen because you didn't really understand the situation.

Solution In Action

When Matt told me his story, he was giving it to me as an example of what happens if you're not meticulous when dealing with Chinese staff people – the incident had happened when Matt was distracted by the visit of an executive from the US. His usual process, he explained, was to go over the details of every production batch, every shipment and every project with the Chinese subordinates involved. He would question each team in person about quality, processes, delivery schedules, and shipping details before allowing things to progress to the next phase. As Matt explained, he always tried to imagine what question he hadn't asked, what thing could go wrong, during these discussions with his subordinates. That process had been extremely successful – they'd had no significant issues until the problem with the Ministry of Commerce came up. Even that problem proved manageable, because he'd budgeted time and money for dealing with unexpected problems of that nature.

Problem # 28 – Hidden Meanings

Understanding Indirect Communications

 Face (perception) is more important than facts (reality)

\+

 Things are better when everyone gets along

\+

 Relationships are more important than rules

= The Chinese communicate in a very indirect way and often avoid saying things directly.

Note: A discussion of indirect communications also appears in Problem # 12 and Problem # 20.

What It's Like

It's like discussing something a friend may be sensitive about (their weight, the fact that they're balding, their age, problems their children are having) - you often talk around the subject, but don't refer to it directly, out of deference to their feelings.

The Problem

The Chinese communicate in a much more indirect way that Westerners, saying things in a soft, often euphemistic way, that allows everyone involved to preserve face, no matter what the outcome of the discussion. This is important in a group-oriented society where the underlying expectation is that at the end of the day, everyone will have to get along and tolerate each other enough to move forward together.

This matters to you because:

1. It's important to be sensitive about potential face issues when talking to a Chinese person,
2. It's important to interpret what a Chinese person is saying in light of the context and
3. It's often just as important to consider what's not said as what is said. In general, this is an area that's fraught with challenges and misunderstandings.

A Story

One of the features of leading a team in China that I was unprepared for was the way they communicated their suggestions in a subtle and roundabout way. In the West my staff described the problems and options and then made recommendations. My Chinese team did the first two steps, but often said nothing about what they recommended. When I expressed frustration about this, one of my Chinese friends explained that they WERE making recommendations, but they were doing it in a completely deniable way, ensuring that neither they nor I would lose face.

For instance, one of my staff people would say, "Options X, Y and Z are all good. R&D favours X. Marketing favours Y. Public Relations favours Z." I then had to infer, based on knowing that the executive in charge of Public Relations held a key position in the power structure, that Z was my staff's preferred option.

Strategies – What You Can Do About It

When dealing with Chinese and their indirect way of communicating, you CAN do the following:

1. <u>Consider the context.</u> When Chinese people are speaking to you, consider the possible meanings of what they're saying, and weigh that in the context of what you know.
2. <u>Beware false positives.</u> Know that Chinese people will rarely tell you anything negative or unpleasant in a direct way – it embarrasses them. They may agree with you even if they think that what you're saying is completely wrong.
3. <u>They think you know what they're talking about.</u> Know that Chinese people think you understand this indirect way of speaking – they think you know what they mean, when often you don't.

Solution In Action

I've found that the main keys to successfully dealing with indirect communications are to watch for non-verbal clues – is the speaker tense or relaxed, smiling or grim? – and to listen hard to any suggestions that are made. I also always try to have a trusted Chinese friend or colleague with me, someone who can advise me on what they believe was said.

Problem # 29 – Unfaithful

Managing Divided Loyalties (Especially To Other Chinese)

 Relationships are more important than rules

+

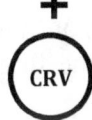 The Cultural Revolution had a massive impact on Chinese society

+

 The long term is what's most important

= The Chinese are more likely to be loyal to other Chinese than to non-Chinese.

What It's Like

It's like immigrant communities, which tend to band together and take their ethnicity as a basis for trust.

The Problem

The Chinese focus on relationships instead of rules, the focus on personal loyalty created by the events of the Cultural Revolution and the long term thinking of Chinese people combine to make them tend to be loyal to other Chinese people more than to non-Chinese people. For Western businesspeople dealing with Chinese counterparts, this often manifests as a mistaken reliance on professionalism – the Westerner believes that the Chinese person will behave with professionalism because of the ongoing business relationship, and is then surprised when the Chinese counterpart's personal loyalties trump professional considerations. To some extent, this is just the Chinese person doing a calculation of who is more likely to help them in the future, a Chinese person or a non-Chinese person.

This matters to you because relying on the wrong assumption is likely to cause you lots of problems when you're working with Chinese people.

A Story

Tony, a Briton working in a Chinese manufacturing company, was surprised to find that one of the Chinese staff in the department Tony had recently taken over was doing work for a Chinese executive in a different department. Tony was outraged at what he saw as the total disloyalty and lack of professionalism of the Chinese subordinate involved – Tony was this subordinate's boss, but the subordinate was taking instruction from another executive! One of Tony's Chinese friends explained that the Chinese staff person was simply looking out for the time when Tony left the company (as he inevitably would), when the Chinese subordinate would need the support of the Chinese executive. The Chinese friend also pointed out that ALL of Tony's Chinese staff were probably doing the same thing, if not as obviously.

Strategies – What You Can Do About It

When dealing with Chinese subordinates and their tendency to have loyalties to others, you CAN do the following:

1. <u>Be aware.</u> Understand that all is not as it seems and that your Chinese counterparts probably DO have other loyalties.
2. <u>Prevent.</u> Do what you can to deny your staff the time or freedom to act for someone else.
3. <u>Make allowance.</u> To the extent possible, try to understand the various loyalties of your subordinates and try not to put them in situations where they have to choose between you and someone else. You may not like the choice they make.

Solution In Action

Following the conversation with his friend, Tony began to keep closer tabs on his staff and what they were doing. He let it be known in various ways that he wouldn't tolerate team members accepting direction from managers in other departments. At the same time, Tony told me that although he loudly demanded that his staff not work for others, and did all he could to make it tough for them to actually do such work, he did nothing to try and catch them at it, for fear of what the fallout would be. In particular, he didn't want to create a situation where the other manager would lose face, or that risked the subordinate on his team leaving his group to go work for the manager in the other department. However, his awareness that these things were going on, and his efforts to make it more difficult to do them, had the desired effect of keeping his staff mostly focused on his tasks.

Problem # 30 – Widely Educated

Managing The Chinese Desire To Develop Themselves Broadly

 Face (perception) is more important than facts (reality)

+

 The long term is what's important

+

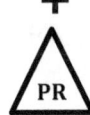 Don't let perfect be the enemy of good enough

 Chinese people aspire to develop themselves broadly, across a number of skill sets and in a number of ways.

What It's Like

It's like a Swiss Army Knife – Chinese professionals want to be self-contained solutions for every problem.

The Problem

In her outstanding 2009 book Factory Girls, Leslie Chang describes a young woman talking to a friend about how to move up in China's new economy:

> "Just try to learn what you can," Min advised. "If you learn something, you can always take it with you to your next job."
>
> "You can only rely on yourself," she concluded.

This encapsulates the view Chinese workers have about their work experience – everything they learn, however obscure or far from their previous training and experience, is likely to help them in the future. They are, therefore, very interested in developing themselves as broadly as possible, in undertaking new roles, even if they're completely unqualified for the job. They want to acquire a large number of skills and competencies in a variety of areas.

This matters to you because:

1. Specialization does not have the same resonance for Chinese people as for Western ones and
2. Chinese people often expect you to have the same desire to acquire diverse skills.

As an aside, an unfortunate manifestation of this desire the Chinese have to broaden themselves is a pervasive practice among Chinese employees and vendors to reverse engineer technologies and processes to which they're exposed. For example, a natural thing to do as part of a manufacturing joint venture would be to explain a critical process to the partner's employees, so that the partner could better understand how to do THEIR job. However, explaining how a process works is likely to go a long way towards giving the partner the knowledge and skills to do it themselves. The Chinese partner may very well take that knowledge, develop their own process based on the information received from their partner, and then use the result to sell the product or service cheaper, thereby undercutting the partner.

See Problem # 18 for a discussion of how to address this issue.

A Story

Something I observe in many companies I work with in China is that people's job assignments are frequently unrelated to their training or experience. More than that, the employees themselves are usually eager to take jobs for which they have no qualifications. For instance, it is very common for an engineer to be in charge of HR, or an accountant to be in sales. When I ask about this, my Chinese friends explain that what the company wants is for the employee to "try their best" and to be willing to start over at the beginning with each new function/assignment. Equally, employees consider getting experience in lots of different disciplines to be a perk in China.

Strategies – What You Can Do About It

When dealing with Chinese subordinates and their desire to broaden their skills sets, you CAN do the following:

1. <u>Don't insist on specialization.</u> Because the Chinese value the idea of having a broad set of skills, specialization sometimes doesn't seem very attractive to them. If you're

employing Chinese people, they will be more energized by gaining broad experience than by specializing.
2. Be flexible. Chinese employees are likely to remain more loyal to an employer who's giving them many opportunities to learn, so be flexible and allow them to do that whenever possible.

Solution In Action

I observe that the most successful people in Chinese companies are those who smilingly accept assignments they know nothing about and are happy to be learning something new. Chinese companies accept the fact that their staff will have broad skill sets, but not deep ones.

Section V

Next Steps

What Happens Next?

"In any moment of decision, the best thing you can do is the right thing, the next best thing is the wrong thing, and the worst thing you can do is nothing."

American President Theodore Roosevelt

The easiest thing to do next is nothing. It's comfortable, it's low energy and it reduces the chance that someone will criticize us for doing the wrong thing. Unfortunately, doing nothing rarely get you where you want to go.

So don't do that! Get stuck in. Get out there and give it a go. Try to ride the dragon and see what happens. Chances are you'll fall off. Sometimes you may feel like you're getting eaten. But you'll get better at it with practice, and you'll be a lot further ahead when the next, even BIGGER Chinese dragon comes your way. Eventually you may even be able to guide the dragon to take you where you want to go.

Here are a few tips that will help:

1. Realize that it will be messy

No matter what you do, the process of trying to deal with someone from another culture is going to be confusing and imperfect. I love China; I speak Chinese; dealing with Chinese businesses is my livelihood; I've lived there and worked for Chinese bosses, half of my customers are Chinese – and I STILL struggle. So relax and don't worry about perfect. Just use the model to try and make the interactions run a little smoother.

2. Know that getting all those wheels to line up is tough

In this book, I've talked about discreet problems and individual cultural elements as if they were chemicals in a laboratory experiment: "Take a 100 grams of hierarchy, add 50 grams of face, stir gently and voila! you have 'Chinese people don't contradict their bosses'." Of course, it doesn't work like that in the real world. You have multiple problems going on at once, many different considerations at play, many different opinions vying for attention. Navigate those crosscurrents as best you can.

3. Remember that individuals are all different

Throughout the book, I've talked about Chinese people as if they were all the same, as if they all behaved in a uniform way. Of course, that's absolutely not the case. China is made up of 1.5 billion individuals, all of whom have their own views, their own history, their own likes and dislikes. Both the most oppressive, micromanaging boss I ever had, and the most open, empowering boss I ever had were Chinese. So individual personalities count for a lot. This book is only giving you an idea of what the average – maybe "stereotypical" would be a better word – Chinese businessperson is like. So don't be afraid to use your judgment in deciding how much of this fits and how much doesn't.

4. Practice, practice, practice

In this case, practice will not make perfect. In the world of intercultural relations, there is no such thing as perfect. But there is good. There's even great. And that comes with practice. Two of the most successful Western executives I know in China both stand out for the fact that they've got no particular Chinese training or background, but they've simply kept working at it over the years.

Keep in mind that if you've got a Chinese investor, colleague or subordinate, you're probably in a relationship that's going to last for some time. You'll have many opportunities to try different things with them, to practice your skills. If the situation turns out badly today, don't worry – there will be a new situation tomorrow.

5. When in doubt, be yourself

There's a lot of stuff in this book that's telling you to act in a way that may seem unnatural. In that respect, it's a bit like manners – we learn to do things in a polite, socially acceptable way, even though that may not be our first impulse.

But good manners – or effective approaches to dealing with your Chinese counterpart – shouldn't be confused with having to be someone you're not.

Probably the best, most widely read book on doing business in China is…wait for it…*Doing Business In China* by Ted Plafker. Plafker, who has lived in China for decades and was the China bureau chief for *The Economist* newspaper, talks about his friend Michael Komersaroff who's an Australian mining specialist working in China. Michael speaks no Chinese, communicates bluntly and to the point, and doesn't even like Chinese food. But he's extremely successful in China because he's sincere and he is a straight dealer. As with anyone, the Chinese pick up on that.

6. Do your best...don't worry about doing more

When I'm worried about how to resolve a particularly thorny problem in China, my friends there constantly remind me, "Just do your best." At first, I thought they were simply being comforting, maybe even a little bit condescending, but I came to see that that's really what they think – you can't do more than your best, and you'll probably be surprised by how much that can achieve. So, quite literally, do your best.

Conclusion

"China is a sleeping giant. Let her sleep, for when she wakes she will move the world."
French General Napoleon Bonaparte

"The lion China has already awakened, but this is a peaceful, pleasant and civilized lion."
Chinese President Xi Jinping

I love China. At a visceral level, I find it fascinating, glamorous, mysterious, dynamic and terrifying.

But whether you love it or hate it, whether you welcome the outbound torrent of Chinese tourists, investors and businesses or fear the erosion of Western power and values, the Chinese are coming. It was always an aberration that a fifth of the world's population sat, quiescent and invisible, within their own borders and with little interest in the outside world. Unless you believe that China will eschew the benefits of international trade and turn inwards on itself, it's inevitable that China and Chinese people will have an ever-greater impact on the world outside.

That being the case, we're all likely to find ourselves with more Chinese business partners, bosses, employees, peers, investors, neighbors, customers and rivals. Which means that it's worth knowing something about how they think, the decisions they make, the values they hold.

How will you deal with the dragon? Will you retreat? Will you hold your own?

Ride the dragon. It may take you somewhere amazing.

How To Reach CT

Participate in a Riding The Dragon Training Course or Mentoring Program.

It's like your own living, breathing, how-to manual on China and the Chinese. If you're already doing business with China, or just starting to think about it, this course will help you approach your Chinese business with greater confidence, clarity and energy.

Follow me at:

Websites: www.ct-johnson.com
              www.crossbordermanagement.com

Twitter: @ctjohnson00

LinkedIn: https://au.linkedin.com/in/christophertoddjohnson

Email: ct.johnson@crossbordermanagement.com

Please don't hesitate to get in touch. I love questions. And I always love to talk about your business in China, or selling to the Chinese.

About The Author

Christopher Todd (CT) Johnson is a thought leader in the field of cross border management. **He helps companies reach foreign clients, win more business in foreign markets, and manage their foreign operations.**

Even more importantly, CT helps his clients develop new ways to communicate their value to foreign customers, opening up new and untapped markets for businesses of all sizes.

CT specializes in sales and management issues between companies in China and the West.

Before starting his consulting practice, CT worked for US consultancy Ernst & Young, Swedish telecom equipment-maker Ericsson, and Chinese electronics giant Huawei Technologies. He has been a board member for several companies in Asia. Professionally, CT's background is in finance and sales. He has a passion for fixing thorny business problems and spent almost a decade doing corporate turnarounds in the US, Russia and Western Europe.

An avid student of language and culture, CT is fluent in German, Russian and Mandarin.

CT lives in Sydney, Australia with his wife, Anne-Marie, and their two children.

www.ingramcontent.com/pod-product-compliance
Lightning Source LLC
Chambersburg PA
CBHW060849170526
45158CB00001B/292